The THINK Series

THINK About

Racism

Linda Mizell

Walker and Company
New York

In memory of Dr. Robert B. Moore, who fought the good fight.

First published in the United States of America in 1992 by Walker Publishing Company, Inc.

Published simultaneously in Canada by Thomas Allen & Son Canada, Limited, Markham, Ontario

Library of Congress Cataloging-in-Publication Data
Mizell, Linda.
    Think about racism / Linda Mizell.
       p.   cm.—(The Think series)
    Includes bibliographical references and index
    Summary: Discusses racism in America and how it has affected history, the law, and contemporary issues.
    ISBN 0-8027-8113-6 (reinforced).
    —ISBN 0-8027-7365-6 (pbk)
    1. Racism—United States—Juvenile literature. 2. United States—Race relations—Juvenile literature.
    [1. Racism. 2. Race relations.] I. Title. II. Series.
    E184.A1M58 1992
    305.8'00973—dc20   91-14575
                                                                CIP
                                                                 AC

Martin Luther King, Jr.'s "*Letter from Birmingham Jail*," in the Appendix, is from *Why We Can't Wait* (New York: Harper & Row, 1964), pp. 77–100. Copyright © 1963, by Martin Luther King, Jr. Reprinted by permission of Harper & Row Publishers.

Printed in the United States of America

10 9 8 7 6 5 4 3 2 1

Special thanks to Dr. Barbara E. Riley, who served as consultant on the manuscript. Dr. Riley is an organizational development consultant specializing in management of diversity, who helps schools, universities, and corporations across the country confront issues of racism and sexism. She is past director of Channels for Educational Choices, a recruitment, referral, and consulting agency to independent schools in New England. She has also served on the board of the Council for Interracial Books for Children.

I wish to acknowledge the invaluable support and assistance of Randy Carter of the National Association of Independent Schools; the Howard Family; the Pisha Family; my colleagues at Cambridge Friends School; the Bethel Women's Fellowship; and my sons, Bakari and Lateef.

CONTENTS

INTRODUCTION

What is racism?

Where did it come from? Has it always been around?

How does racism differ from prejudice, bigotry, and discrimination?

Is racism a "natural" tendency?

If racism is bad, why does it continue to exist?

These are some of the questions that this book will help you think about. Most books for young people don't discuss topics that are unpleasant—topics like racism—because many adults assume that younger readers "can't handle it." Usually, though, the best way to "handle" unpleasantness is not to ignore it, but to know the facts and to learn some ways to change it.

Racism is not a simple subject, and to understand it you must know the facts. Contrary to what some people believe, there is nothing "natural" about racism. It didn't just spring up all by itself out of nowhere. The story of racism is the story of many people, many events—events involving conquest and riches, fear and greed—and many ideas about them. This book will tell you about some of these people, events, and ideas, so that you can think about why racism exists and what you can and should do about it.

One of the first questions that comes to mind is: what is race, anyway? Is race really based on biological differences?

In the United States, most people think of race in

terms of physical characteristics such as skin color, hair texture, and features. But what about the black person with "white" skin and straight hair, or the white person with dark skin and full lips? And what about people of mixed race? It's estimated that one in every five white Americans has African ancestors. A 1930 study concluded that more than 70 percent of American blacks had white ancestors, nearly 30 percent had Indian ancestors, and only 22 percent were of unmixed African ancestry.

Race is more than skin color or even a set of physical characteristics. It is how people define themselves or others as part of a specific group. In the United States (and in some other countries as well) it is one measure by which privileges are accorded. Many of our customs and laws are based on our negative attitudes about what we define as race. These attitudes, customs, and laws can be defined as racism.

People often say *racism* when what they really mean is *prejudice* or *discrimination*. All three terms are related—but different. Let's look at some real incidents that illustrate these differences.

Sylvia and Kathy have just learned that one of their classmates, Maria, won't be returning to school this year because she's pregnant. "Well, what do you expect?" Sylvia says. "After all, she's Puerto Rican. My mother says those people have babies like cats have kittens. Besides, she was too dumb to make it here anyway."

Prejudice means to *pre-judge*, to form an opinion about someone or something without knowing the facts. Prejudice has to do with feelings and attitudes. When you have negative feelings about someone simply because that person is different from you, that's prejudice.

When you dislike someone or make judgments about her because of her race, that's racial prejudice. Racial prejudice means having positive feelings about your own race and negative feelings about others. Anyone, from any race or ethnic group, can be prejudiced. When Sylvia talked about Maria, she was expressing her prejudices. Her prejudices were based on stereotypes—deciding that all "those people" are alike (and morally inferior)—which her mother believed.

Sam and his friend Bobby decide to answer an ad for baggers in the supermarket near their school. Sam has a make-up test after school, though, and Bobby can't wait for him because he has a dentist appointment later that afternoon. When Sam arrives at the store, he's given an application to fill out. The manager talks with him, then tells him he can start the next day because they're really shorthanded. That night, he calls Bobby to tell him the good news, thinking how much fun they'll have working together. Sam is stunned to learn that when Bobby went to the supermarket, he was told that all the jobs had been filled.

"Why would they do that?" Sam wonders.

"Probably because I'm black and that neighborhood is white," Bobby answers. "It wouldn't be the first time. It's just never happened to you because you're white."

Discrimination has to do with behavior. When you base your decisions or actions on your prejudices, as the manager of the store did, you are discriminating. Bobby was the victim of a special kind of discrimination. When racial prejudice is combined with the power to discriminate against any and all members of that group, it's called *racism*.

Even though Sam wasn't responsible for the store manager's feelings or actions, he did benefit from them. When a system such as a school, court, or even a supermarket is set up to provide advantages to one group of people at the expense of another, it's called *institutional racism*.

Racism exists because of the acts of many individuals who either make and carry out discriminatory practices, or who allow them to continue. Although anyone can be prejudiced and can discriminate as an individual, a person must belong to the group that has institutional power in order to be racist.

Thung and her family came to the United States three years ago. The first year was very difficult for Thung, but she worked hard to learn English and get good grades in school. Last week, Thung learned that she had won a full scholarship to a very prestigious private school. Just yesterday, it was announced in the local newspaper. Several people congratulated her; others seemed angry, including some girls who had always been friendly to her before. This morning Thung arrived at school to find a note taped to her locker that contained racial slurs and the message, "We're sick of you people taking everything from us—why don't you go back where you came from!"

Some people think that racism results from thinking that you're better or smarter than other people. That's not always true. Sometimes, a person may behave in a racist way out of fear that he may not be as good or as smart as someone else. Many Asian-Americans have experienced this kind of racism.

Last year, Mike led his team to the regional football championship. He set new school records for total yards rushing and passes completed. The voting for most valuable player was by secret ballot, but afterward almost everyone on the team told Mike that they had voted for him. You can imagine how surprised they all were when another kid was named MVP. Mike learned later that the coach had been pressured to rig the vote; a wealthy alumnus was about to make a big contribution, and some of the school's trustees were afraid that he would change his mind if the team's MVP *was* black.

Most people assume that you must hate someone or intentionally hurt them because of their race in order to be racist. That certainly wasn't the case with Mike's coach. In fact, the coach liked Mike a lot and would never intentionally do anything to hurt him. But the fact remains that by carrying out the orders of the trustees, he discriminated against Mike for being black. One important thing to remember is that intention is not a necessary ingredient in racism. It is the *effect* of a law, practice, or behavior that determines whether or not it is racist.

After the passage of the Fifteenth Amendment, which guaranteed the right to vote to all men regardless of race, color, or previous condition of servitude, southern states passed voting laws that contained literacy, property, or tax requirements. Exceptions were made for people whose ancestors had voted prior to the Civil War. This exception of course didn't apply to blacks, because between the mid-1700s and 1867, whether free or enslaved, they were not allowed to vote in any southern states.

In this case, although none of these laws specifically mentioned race, their intent clearly was to discriminate against blacks.

The history of racism in the United States is, to a great extent, the history of people of color. It was the growth of American slavery and the transatlantic slave trade that prompted the development of the concept of racism. It was the economic exploitation of blacks, Native Americans, Latinos, and Asians that continued to breed racism. Throughout the history of this nation, racial discrimination has been embedded in our fundamental laws as well as our common practices.

And so, to understand racism in today's society, we must look back to our history to trace its beginnings. That is what we'll do in the next several chapters.

REVIEW QUESTIONS

1. Is race a scientific concept?
2. What is institutional racism?
3. Can a person be prejudiced without being racist?

1 Race in the Early Americas

When and how did the concept of race begin? How was race used to justify conquest and slavery?

What was it like to be a child in 1492? That depends a lot on what part of the world you lived in. If you were white, there's a good chance that you lived somewhere in Europe in a poor cottage and helped your family farm someone else's land. If you were black, you might have lived in the prosperous African empire of Songhay, where education was highly valued, and where boys probably spent at least part of their day in taking lessons. If you're Latino, your Indian and Spanish ancestors had not yet met.

By 1492, Africa and Asia had been trading both goods and ideas for centuries. After years of struggling among themselves, the countries of Europe were now looking past their continental borders in hopes of gaining the riches that their African and Asian neighbors seemed to possess in abundance. And the two large continents to the west, soon to be called the Americas, had not yet come into sustained contact with the "Old World." (Occasional visitors from the coast of Guinea had been there and left behind fragments of West African language and culture along with their images in clay, gold, and stone, but this fact wasn't widely known or accepted in Europe.)

COLUMBUS AND THE "INDIOS"

When Christopher Columbus embarked on his first voyage, he was hoping to discover a western route to India and the Far East. His more important mission, however, was to find gold and other precious goods. What he found instead was the island now called San Salvador, where the friendly Taino people swam out to meet him.

Columbus and his men were greeted warmly with food, water, and gifts, as was the custom among the Taino and other Arawakan people. Columbus repaid their hospitality by kidnapping ten of them. Thinking he really had reached India, he named San Salvador and the nearby islands the Indies. He called the people there Indios. At every stop, the first question he asked the Indians was, "Where is the gold?"

Columbus never found gold in these islands, at least not in large quantities. Instead of going back empty-handed, he offered the kidnapped Indians to the Spanish monarchs as curious gifts. On his second voyage, he brought 500 enslaved Arawakan people back to Spain. Two hundred of them died on the way.

Those who were left behind were forced into slavery, too. In the Cicao province of Haiti, everyone fourteen years of age or older had to bring the Spaniards a certain amount of gold every three months. Those who failed had their hands cut off. When all the gold had been found, the people were forced to work on large plantations. Many of them died from the hard work. Those who tried to run away were hunted down and killed. When the Arawaks tried to organize an army to fight back, they were hanged or burned to death.

Modern historians estimate that there were 250,000 Arawak people in 1492. By 1515, there were perhaps 50,000. By 1550, there were 500, and by 1650, none.

A NEW SOURCE OF SILVER AND GOLD

This brutal pattern was repeated over and over again as Europeans came to the New World. Other Spanish expeditions came to present-day South and Central America, where there really were large deposits of

European conquerers treated New World natives with vicious brutality. (Courtesy of The Library of Congress)

both gold and silver. In the beginning, the *conquistadores* (as the Spanish were called) were welcomed with extravagant gifts of precious metals. These riches inspired them to ransom their hosts or to destroy or enslave entire communities in order to get more.

By the mid-1500s, the Spanish controlled gold and silver mines all over South America. After a rich silver deposit was discovered in Bolivia, 6,000 Africans were brought to mine the ore, but they soon died from the brutal work in the unfamiliar high altitude. The native people were then forced to work in the mines without pay. Because the labor needed to extract them was free, these precious metals became plentiful in Europe. Until then, only royalty and the rich aristocracy possessed gold and silver. Now, for the first time, there was enough money in circulation, especially silver, that others had some, too. In fact, large amounts of American silver made it possible for the traditional mercantile system of Europe to become a money economy.

In 1600, the gold and silver in Europe totaled $1.6 billion, eight times as much as there had been before Europeans first came to the Americas. From 1500 to 1650, between 180 and 200 tons of gold alone went to Europe from the Americas. Today that gold would be worth close to $3 billion. Because gold was so plentiful, much of it went to adorn churches, public buildings, and the homes of the rich, where it can still be seen today. Very little of it is left in the countries where it was first mined.

Before the European invasion of the Americas, most of the world's gold had come from West Africa. One ruler of Ghana, an African country that dominated the western Sudan until the eleventh century, was said to have owned a gold nugget so big that a horse could be tethered to it. For centuries, wealthy and powerful African nations traded gold for cloth, beads, craftwork, and other European goods. The long trade routes across the Sahara, which passed goods from merchant to merchant, were very slow, though, and made gold precious and hard for Europeans to come by.

By all accounts, the African kingdom of Mali was one of the greatest empires of the fourteenth century, followed by Songhay in the fifteen and sixteen centuries. In the 1500s the city of Timbuktu was Songhay's center of intellectual life and culture. People from Europe and other parts of the world came there to study history, law, and medicine. Successful cataract operations and other kinds of surgery were performed by Africans. One visitor reported that the book trade was more profitable than any other business.

Once the New World became Europe's major source of gold, the ancient African trade routes were no longer profitable. As commerce declined, so did the intellectual and social exchange. The great African empires declined and were soon forgotten. Instead of gold, Europe now looked to Africa for slaves. The Indians of the Caribbean who had once been enslaved to work the colonial plantations had long since been killed off. Indians brought from other parts of the continent soon died from tropical diseases like malaria and yellow fever. As more plantations were established to the north, the European demand for slave labor grew.

SLAVERY AND THE SLAVE TRADE

The institution of slavery was not new. It had existed throughout human history, in almost every century, in almost every culture. Slavery was so common that, according to the ancient Greek philosopher Plato, everyone has slave ancestors. Blacks were known all over the world, including Europe. Some had come to Europe as slaves. But until the eleventh century, people were enslaved mainly because of war. During the Crusades, Christians and Moslems used religion to justify slavery. In the fifteenth century, race became the primary basis for slavery.

In 1444, Henry the Navigator, prince of Portugal, sent ships to explore the coast of Africa. His men brought back African captives, who were sold into slavery. By 1455, 1,000 enslaved Africans were brought to Portugal each year. A hundred years later, in some parts of Portugal there were more blacks than whites. But Africans were not seen as inferior because of skin color, and their status as slaves was not necessarily inherited by their children. When the Portuguese and Spanish set out for the New World, descendants of those Africans went with them.

While the Spanish concentrated on establishing planting colonies and mining precious metals, the English took on the job of supplying them with slaves. At the same time, they pirated the Spaniards' ill-gotten shipments of gold and goods.

If Europeans had not stumbled upon the Americas, the African slave trade might never have grown very large. But the sparsely populated land, with its promise of unlimited riches, could not be exploited without vast amounts of labor. And the cheaper the labor, the greater the profits.

The Spanish had already reduced much of the South and Central American native population to slavery and impoverishment, or in many cases, death from disease and brutal working conditions. In the sixteenth century, they began bringing enslaved Africans to the coastal areas in large numbers. The trickle of slaves from Africa to Europe was diverted to America. By the end of the next century it had turned into a flood.

By 1553, there were 20,000 enslaved Africans in Mexico alone. When the supply of gold and silver was exhausted almost a hundred years later, the English abandoned piracy and turned to trade exclusively. The African slave trade was their major undertaking.

By then the English had begun to establish their own colonies along the Eastern Seaboard, through trading companies chartered by King James. When Jamestown was first settled in 1607, it was to serve as a permanent trade center. The same is true of almost every other European settlement in the Western Hemisphere.

The North American colonies soon abandoned the idea of using Indians as slaves for agricultural work. The Indians were more familiar with the land than the English were and could easily run away. Since the colonists were surrounded by and outnumbered by the Indians, it was foolish to risk war unnecessarily. Besides, it was far more profitable to depend on them for the fur trade.

If valuable trade goods such as furs and tobacco were not available in large enough quantities, the companies cultivated crops as a last resort. Servants indentured for seven years, convicts, and the companies' own contract laborers—virtually all of them white—were brought to the colonies along with captive Africans to work the plantations. Other Africans came to the colonies as indentured servants. A few came on their own.

Individual prejudices did exist in the early colonies, especially among the wealthy. However, discrimination was usually based more on *class* than on race. Poor people of any color were considered inferior to rich people. Legally, there was little or no distinction between slaves and servants. Until 1630 there was not even a clear definition of the term *slave*. Until the late 1600s, blacks were referred to in public records as *servants*.

At first, both white and black servants were treated equally. All of them were overworked, underfed, beaten, brutalized, and treated with contempt. Often, their common suffering brought them together. It was not at all unusual for them to socialize together, attempt to run away together, or to marry each other. After finishing their terms of service, many blacks went on to acquire property, vote, hold office, testify in court, and sometimes have servants of their own.

Things changed in the 1660s when Europe began to clamor for North American crops such as cotton, rice, and tobacco. The demand for labor in the colonies that produced these crops exceeded the supply. White Europeans were only coming in small numbers, but the supply of African slaves seemed limitless. By then over one million enslaved Africans had already been brought to Spanish and Portuguese colonies in South America and the Caribbean. The

English colonies decided that African slavery was the answer to their problems, too.

Why slavery instead of a continued mix of servants and slaves? Africans were considered stronger and more adaptable than Indians or Europeans. It was cheaper to buy a slave outright than to hire the services of a European for seven years. Many Africans already possessed valuable agricultural skills. Because their native climate was in some ways similar to the climate of the coastal colonies, they were often immune to the tropical diseases that afflicted the transplanted English. Differences in race and language made it hard for a runaway African to blend into a crowd the same way an escaped white servant could. And whites, whatever their legal status, were still under the protection of recognized European governments. Mistreatment or enslavement of whites could cause economic and political problems for the colonists.

THE EXTERMINATION OF INDIANS

Just as the colonists decided that slavery would be the fate of Africans, so they decided that extinction would be the fate of Indians. When each of the English settlements began, the Indians of that area were friendly and helpful, and many times saved the colonists from starvation. Often, though, the English would attack the Indians on the slightest excuse, killing men, women, and children and burning their homes and crops. In 1622, one official wrote that "the way of conquering them is much more easie then of civilizing them by faire meanes."

During the terrible winter of 1610 when the starving Jamestown colonists dug up corpses for food, some of them ran off to live among an Indian tribe. That summer, the Indians refused to return the runaways. To punish them, the English destroyed another Indian settlement and brutally killed the people there.

As more and more English immigrants arrived, they took more and more Indian land. Sometimes they obtained it by trade or trickery, but more often by killing the Indians who lived there. Fifty-five years after the Pilgrims landed at Plymouth Rock, the Pequot, the Wampanoags, and the Narragansett—people who had once numbered in the thousands—were virtually exterminated. Those who were not killed by war died from diseases brought by Europeans. And the captives of war were sold into slavery in the Caribbean.

For the European adventurers, the theft of land and labor was sure to lead to vast wealth; the problem was how to justify the immoral enslavement of one group of people and the extermination of another to obtain that wealth.

The answer was to develop the idea of racism.

THE DEVELOPMENT OF RACISM

Most people find it hard to be deliberately cruel to other people—because of their religious beliefs, their moral convictions, or because they value human dignity and life. The same must have been true of the Europeans who were profiting from the enslavement of Africans and the killing of Indians.

The conflict between morality and greed is one reason that racism developed. Europeans needed to convince themselves that other races were somehow less than human in order to justify the brutal and inhumane—but ultimately profitable—acts committed against them.

Over the next hundred years, the theologians, scientists, and intellectuals of northern, industrial Europe (along with their European counterparts in the Americas) wrote and argued about race, skin color, and nationality. Despite their areas of disagreement, they all agreed on two points: that the fair nordic Europeans ("Aryans") were by far the most superior race of all, and that the dark-skinned Africans and their descendants ("Ethiopians") were the most inferior, with Asians and Indians only slightly higher above blacks on the scale.

On the basis of these assumptions, Europeans continued to fight among themselves over their "divine and natural" right to conquer, dominate, and exploit the Americas and the rest of the world.

REVIEW QUESTIONS

1. What was the major difference between ancient slavery and modern slavery?
2. Have dark-skinned people always been considered inferior?
3. How was Columbus greeted by the people he called Indios? How did he respond to them? Was this pattern repeated as other Europeans came to North America?
4. In the early American colonies, were all blacks slaves? Were all slaves black?
5. Did slaves and white servants mix socially in the colonies?

2 Racism and the Law: From Colonies to the New Republic

How did racism become part of our fundamental laws?

What role did wealth and property play in shaping the law?

How were laws and government policies used to reinforce racism?

EARLY SLAVERY LAWS

In 1641, Massachusetts became the first colony to pass laws establishing slavery. Other colonies soon followed. Under these new laws, race determined a person's legal status. Blacks were made slaves for life. Babies born to a slave mother would also be slaves, even if their father were free. Under these laws, Africans became property to the Europeans instead of fellow human beings.

One of the first reasons given for legalizing African slavery was religion. Most Europeans believed that it was their divine right (or even duty) as Christians to conquer and enslave other people who weren't. They considered Africans to be "heathens." Many of the slave ships had Christian names such as *Jesus* and *John the Baptist*.

However, many of the Africans arrived in the colonies as Christians. Many more became Christians later. Whenever the Spanish, Portuguese, and French colonies claimed an area, one of the first things they did was to build a church. Sometimes the priests were explorers. Bartolomé de las Casas was a Spanish priest who helped conquer Cuba. He urged that Indian slaves be replaced by blacks, because he thought that blacks could better withstand the cruelties of slavery. Later, he changed his mind and began a crusade to end all slavery. He was hated by many of his compatriots for his beliefs. Sadly, his writings were often misused to justify African slavery.

Church leaders argued over whether it was a sin to baptize slaves or to enslave fellow Christians. In the early days of the English colonies, blacks sometimes testified in court against whites because they had been baptized as Christians. In 1667, the Virginia Assembly declared that baptism had nothing to do with whether a person was enslaved or free. And other colonies passed laws that stated that a person could be both a Christian and a slave.

Not everyone agreed with these laws. In 1688, a group of Quakers in Germantown, Pennsylvania made the first recorded protest against African slavery. They said that slave trafficking was sinful and "worse for them which say they are Christians."

Virginia and Maryland passed many other laws that defined slavery and the status of blacks. Blacks were prevented from marrying whites. They could not own property or weapons, testify against whites, vote, or hold office. It was against the law for an African to strike a white person, even in self-defense. There were laws against educating Africans and against Africans assembling. African religions were outlawed. In some places it was illegal to speak African languages. The purpose of these laws was to keep blacks under tight control.

DEALING WITH RUNAWAYS AND UPRISINGS

The slaveholders were afraid of slave revolts—and with good reason. Enslaved Africans were willing to risk their lives for their freedom. The slaveholders didn't want blacks to have any chances to organize themselves. They passed laws intended to make the slaves afraid to fight. Blacks could be punished with whipping, branding, and cutting off body parts. They could be put to death by hanging, burning, and dismemberment. These brutal laws were called the *Slave Codes*. Many of them also applied to free blacks and to Indians.

From the beginning, enslaved Africans resisted by running away. Sometimes they formed bands of *outlyers* or joined with the Indians. The outlyers often harassed the slave plantations and helped rescue other captives. Runaways from the South Carolina plantations frequently made their way to Spanish Florida. In the early 1700s, white planters on the southern frontiers were constantly on guard against attacks by blacks and Indians from the Florida Territories.

Other laws forbade free blacks to travel in Indian country, or required Indians to return runaway black slaves. Whites in the southern colonies were outnumbered by both blacks and Indians, and so the colonial governments tried to keep them away from each other.

There were fewer slaves in the northern colonies, but their situation was not much better than that of slaves in the South. Uprisings by groups of Africans and Indians were common. In 1657, one group destroyed some buildings in Hartford, Connecticut. In 1708, a black woman was burned alive, and two black and one Indian male slaves were hanged for their participation in a slave revolt on Long Island, New York. Similar incidents happened in other northern colonies.

Even before laws were written that applied only to blacks, the existing laws were not applied equally. In 1640, when six servants in Virginia tried to run away, the one black among them was given thirty lashes and branded on the cheek with the letter *R*. From then on, he was shackled while he worked. He was given an extra year or more of service. The five whites received lighter sentences. Whites were often punished with extra years of service. For the same offenses, black servants might be bound to their masters for life.

One reason the laws were unfairly applied was to discourage black and white servants from treating each other as equals and from working together against their masters. There were special penalties for whites who ran away with blacks. White servants who married blacks or Indians, whether slave or free, were punished with extra years of servitude. Free white men or women were fined, jailed, or forced into servitude. In Maryland, a 1664 law declared that any white woman who married a slave would become a slave for her husband's lifetime, and that their children would also be slaves.

There are many documented cases of white bonded servants and other poor whites uniting with blacks against the landowners. The largest and most famous was led by Nathaniel Bacon in 1676. Bacon himself was not poor. He owned land and had been elected to the Virginia House of Burgesses.

Bacon's Rebellion united poor blacks and whites, both free and enslaved. Tragically, their anger over the government's policies was turned against the Indians. Bacon and his followers first attacked and destroyed Indian settlements and then took control of Jamestown. They passed laws that favored the poor (six out of seven people in Virginia). They gave the right to vote to free men, both black and white (but not Indian). The wealthy planters regained control several months later after Bacon died, but some of his government's reforms remained in force for decades.

Bacon's Rebellion showed the wealthy planters that they could no longer rely on poor whites for forced labor. As a result, the planters began to import African slaves in much greater numbers. Poor whites who had once worked in the planters' fields became even poorer. They began to resent the enslaved black workers.

The slaveholders took advantage of these racial feelings by organizing landless whites into slave patrols. These patrols monitored the movement of blacks. They brutalized those who were found off the plantations without permission. The patrols were given legal authority by the Slave Codes.

THE SLAVE TRADE AND THE AMERICAN REVOLUTION

Over the next one hundred years the slave trade flourished. The number of African slaves in the English colonies grew to half a million. In 1713, England and Spain signed the *Assiento*. This agreement gave England the right to supply Spanish America with slaves for the next thirty years. By the time the American Revolution began, every European colony in North America held Africans as slaves.

The English dominated the African slave trade, but American colonies also took part. Shipbuilders provided the vessels for transporting goods and slaves. Distilleries took the sugar cane that slaves grew and turned it into rum, which was traded for more slaves. By the 1700s, and throughout the century, most of New England's industries depended on slavery.

CASH!

**All persons that have SLAVES to dispose of, will do
well by giving me a call, as I will give the**

HIGHEST PRICE FOR

Men, Women, &

CHILDREN.

Any person that wishes to sell, will call at Hill's tavern, or at Shannon Hill for me, and any information they want will be promptly attended to.

Thomas Griggs.

Charlestown, May 7, 1835.

PRINTED AT THE FREE PRESS OFFICE, CHARLESTOWN.

The American colonies were willing and eager partners in the African slave trade. Still, the First Continental Congress declared in 1774 that the American colonies would no longer take part in the slave trade after the following December, nor trade with others who did. That declaration was soon forgotten. Two years later, in the first draft of the Declaration of Independence, Thomas Jefferson condemned the English king's "cruel war against human nature itself, violating its most sacred rights of life and liberty in the person of a distant people who never offended him, captivating and carrying them into slavery in another hemisphere, or to incur miserable death in their transportation thither."

Jefferson was not concerned about the welfare of captive Africans. He himself owned hundreds of slaves until his death. His real concern was that King George was offering freedom to slaves who joined the British side. Jefferson was protesting the loss of "property" and the threat to slaveholders' lives. That passage was removed from the final draft because the signers of the Declaration of Independence, some of whom were slaveholders, disagreed among themselves about ending the slave trade.

In 1777, Vermont became the first American colony to abolish slavery, followed by Massachusetts and New Hampshire. Meanwhile, the southern slave population was still growing. At the height of the Revolutionary War, the South Carolina militia was too busy keeping slaves under control to engage in the war effort. Lured by the promise of freedom, tens of thousands of blacks, many of them runaways, fought on the side of the British. When the British withdrew, 20,000 blacks went with them. Only 5,000 fought with the American colonists. Nearly all of the Indian nations that took sides in the Revolutionary War also joined with the British.

LAWS IN THE NEW NATION

When the British lost the war, the Indians continued to fight. Americans continued to take their land. Four years later in 1787, the Continental Congress passed the Northwest Ordinance, which promised that the land and property of Indians would never be taken away without their consent. The ordinance also forbade slavery in the Northwest territory. Neither promise was kept. That same year, the protection of slavery was written into federal law.

After the war, very little had changed in the lives of ordinary people. The new constitutions drawn up by the states were very much like the old ones. All but Pennsylvania continued to require that free men own property in order to vote or hold office. The new central government created in 1781 under the Articles of Confederation had very little power, and the majority of common people preferred it that way.

The war had been fought mostly by poor men. Instead of the pay they were expecting, they received certificates for future redemption. Many of the small farmers returned home in debt, ending up in court. Many cruel evictions took place. In 1786–87, hundreds of armed farmers led by Daniel Shays protested by forcing the western Massachusetts courts to close. More farmers and even soldiers joined them, and other confrontations followed. The frightened merchants of Boston raised and paid for an army that eventually put down the rebellion.

Shays's Rebellion raised troubling issues for the wealthy elites. Merchants saw that the central government was not strong enough to protect their financial interests. Slaveholders saw that there was no army to stop slave rebellions as British troops had done before the war. They solved their problems with the U.S. Constitution.

The fifty-five men who wrote the Constitution were all merchants, slaveholders, or property owners. They believed that government should be controlled by the wealthy, and that the first object of government should be the protection of their property.

The Constitution protected the slave trade from legislation for at least twenty years. It also set federal taxes on the import of African slaves. It gave slave-owners the right to track down fugitive slaves across state lines and promised that federal troops would be used to put down slave revolts. When southerners and northerners argued over how to count enslaved Africans for taxation and representation, they compromised by counting each slave as three-fifths of a person.

None of these clauses ever used the word *slave* or mentioned race. Instead, slaves are referred to as "person[s] held to Service or Labour" (Article IV, Section 2, Clause 3) or as "other Persons" (Article I, Section 2, Clause 3).

The Constitution also provided for the "orderly" settlement of Indian lands west of the Appalachians. In 1789, the secretary of war offered two possible solutions to the "Indian problem." One was to exterminate the Indians. The other was to form treaties and punish the whites who broke them. He repeated the promise of the Northwest Ordinance that Indian

The rights of the Indians to their lands will not now or ever be abridged by the people of the United States of America.

Signed, Congress

land should not be taken without the consent of the Indians. He added, though, that it could be taken "by the right of conquest in case of a just war."

In the years that followed, Congress continued to pass laws that guaranteed the rights of Indians. Of course, whenever white settlers moved westward, a "just war" would be started against the Indians. Then the laws would be changed again, until the next time the growing nation became greedy for more Indian lands.

REVIEW QUESTIONS

1. Why did the colonies pass special laws pertaining to blacks and Indians? Did these groups receive harsher punishments than whites?

2. Did a passage in the first draft of the Declaration of Independence condemn or support slavery? Why was that passage later taken out?

3. In what four ways did the Constitution protect slavery?

3 | Western Expansion, Eastern Encroachment

Why was the fate of Indians and enslaved blacks inseparable?

In what ways was race an issue in the westward expansion of the mid-1800s?

How did issues of race, conscience, and economics push the United States into civil war?

BATTLES OVER INDIAN LANDS: 1750s to 1813

In 1802, white slaveholders all over the Americas were talking about Napoleon's crushing defeat by former slaves on the island of Santo Domingo. Toussaint L'Ouverture and his black army had routed the French army and renamed their country Haiti. In 1805, Napoleon ended his New World ventures by selling 885,000 square miles of Indian lands to the United States in a deal known as the Louisiana Purchase.

Thomas Jefferson was then the president of the

United States. He had already committed the government to removing the Creek and the Cherokee from their lands in Florida. His plan was to encourage them to move into the Louisiana Territory, take up farming, trade with whites, get into debt, and then sell their lands to pay off these debts.

Indians had fought to protect their homelands from the Spanish, the French, and the British. When the Europeans fought among themselves, some tribes tried to remain neutral. That wasn't always possible, since the Europeans were usually fighting over Indian lands. Other tribes joined whichever side it seemed would best protect their interests.

In the 1750s and 1760s, several Indian nations fought with the French (who called it the Seven Years' War) against the British (who considered it part of the French and Indian Wars). When the French gave up in 1760, the Indians did not. From 1763 to 1766 a group of eighteen nations, led by an Ottawa chief named Pontiac, tried to drive the British out of their lands once and for all. The British responded by issuing the Proclamation of 1763, which said that whites could not purchase Indian property or settle west of the Appalachian Mountains. Whites who had already settled there were ordered to move out.

The British thought that this solution would do more than just end the war with the Indians. It would also restrict the colonies to a smaller geographical area, making them more dependent on British goods and easier to control. But the British misjudged the Americans. Speculators continued to make land deals in the outlawed territories, just as white settlers continued to cross the mountains. Pontiac's Rebellion continued for another two years, followed by others.

As for the American colonists, they were angry. After the French and Indian Wars, they had expected to be able to settle freely wherever they chose. Land-holders like George Washington and Patrick Henry were especially concerned, because they "owned" large amounts of land in Indian territory. Dissatisfaction with these restrictions, along with the heavy taxes required to pay for the French and Indian Wars, helped lead to the American war for independence from Britain.

By 1812, the United States and Great Britain were again at war over Indian lands in Canada, in Florida, and in the West. During the War of 1812, many Indian nations and leaders again allied themselves with the British.

One of them was a Shawnee chief named Tecumtha, who lived near the Ohio River. He was known to the whites as Tecumseh, and that is how he is referred to in most history books. Tecumtha believed that all Indian land belonged to all Indian people, and that no one had a right to sell any of it. He believed that in order to protect their lands from the white invaders, Indians would have to fight them as one nation instead of many. His brother Laulewaskia preached that Indians should abandon the ways of the white man, especially vices such as alcohol, and return to their traditional ways. Together they traveled all over Indian territory to spread this message of Indian pride and unity.

When the United States declared war on Britain in 1812, it was clear to Tecumtha that if the British won, Indians would be able to keep at least part of their lands; but if the United States won, all Indian lands would eventually be taken away. He chose to fight on the British side. War parties from many nations joined him. While leading the fighting in the Northwest, he encouraged the southern tribes to unite in battle. The Creek Confederation did fight against the Americans in the South. They were defeated when other Creek and Cherokee helped the whites in exchange for promises of friendship. Deserted by the British and greatly outnumbered, Tecumtha and his men were also defeated. He died in 1813 in the battle of Thames River.

INDIAN "REMOVAL" FROM THE SOUTH

Following their defeat in the South, hundreds of Creek known as "Red Sticks" fled to Florida. Thousands of black fugitives also continued to go there. The British recruited these two groups. The Creek were promised their own lands; the blacks were promised their freedom and land in either Florida or the British West Indies.

Meanwhile, General Andrew Jackson, who had become a popular hero during the war, was appointed treaty commissioner. He forced on the Creek a treaty that took away half of their land. He even took away the land of those Creek who had fought with him. Over the next decade, he took most of Alabama and Florida and much of Tennessee, Georgia, Mississippi, Kentucky, and North Carolina.

After encouraging white settlers to move into their lands, Jackson would tell the Indians that the government could not control the settlers. The Indians would be promised safety if they moved elsewhere. But as soon as they did, they would again be forced to give up their lands.

The British withdrew in 1815, leaving their former allies armed and in control of a fort called Prospect Bluff. It was one of the newest and best forts the British had built. It overlooked the Apalachicola River on the southwest coast of Florida. Escaped blacks continued to pour into Florida from as far away as Tennessee and joined numerous communities of Seminole Indians.

These communities angered white slaveholders, whose settlements moved farther and farther into Seminole territory. The Indians frequently launched attacks against the whites. In the process they helped even more slaves to escape.

Jackson began leading raids against the Seminoles to root out runaway slaves and unfriendly Indians. What was even more important to him was acquiring the Florida Territories. He claimed that this military campaign, called the Seminole War of 1818 (or the First Seminole War), was in self-defense. He insisted that the domination of Florida was essential to U.S. security.

After a year of warfare, Spain sold Florida to the United States. Jackson became governor of the Florida Territories. The Seminoles were pushed to the interior, and the coastal areas were opened to white settlement and plantation slavery.

The Bureau of Indian Affairs was created by Congress in 1824. It was a section of the War Department. Instead of dealing fairly with the Indians, the Indian Bureau was used to take Indian land.

Jackson was elected president in 1828. In 1829, gold was discovered in Georgia, on Cherokee land. In 1830, Congress passed the Indian Removal Act, which forced at least 75,000 Indians from the eastern tribes to give up their lands and move to reservations west of the Mississippi River in what was designated "Indian Territory" by the U.S. government.

By then, most of the northern Indian nations had been nearly wiped out, but the southern nations still owned some of the richest land in the South. Their removal would mean huge profits for land speculators. It would also open the way for huge cotton plantations.

Most northern politicians were against removal. Senator Theodore Frelinghuysen of New Jersey asked his fellow senators, "Do the obligations of justice change with the color of the skin?" Others, especially southerners, favored the measure, calling it "the greatest question that ever came before Congress."

The bill narrowly passed both Houses. Except for war, the federal government had never before organized such a massive undertaking. Most of their attention focused on the "Five Civilized Tribes" of the South, so called because they had adopted some white notions of civilization. They were the Cherokee, Choctaw, Chickasaw, Creek, and Seminoles.

According to the law, the tribes had to give their consent in order to be moved. As it turned out, many tribes were forced to leave whether they consented or not; with others, consent was obtained by trickery or threat.

Southern states passed laws that gave them control over Indians, even though only the federal government had the right to pass such laws. Tribal meetings were outlawed, and chiefs were stripped of their powers. Indian lands were distributed by state lotteries to white settlers. It was illegal for Indians to speak against migration, even to one another. The Cherokee were forbidden to mine for gold on their own lands, although whites continued to do so. Indians could not employ white men. Many other laws made it nearly impossible for Indians to live normal lives.

Indians accused of breaking one of these laws lost all property rights. The same tactics were used against tribes to break previous treaties. Indian settlements were attacked. The people were robbed, beaten, raped, and driven from their homes. Their properties were seized. Liquor was even sold from their churches. Wild game was destroyed so that there would be food shortages.

Sometimes individual Indians signed treaties, based on bribes and promises that the government had no intention of keeping. Even though such individual agreements were against Indian tradition and law, whole tribes were forced to move. Those who refused were chained and marched away at gunpoint.

"Removal" was in fact a polite name for a brutal process. Private contractors were hired by the army to oversee the process. Although the contractors were paid well, the Indians were not given adequate food, blankets, or medical care. The young, the old, and the sick were herded away in wagons and on foot. They crossed the Mississippi River in overcrowded, rotting boats. Over 300 Creek died when an old steamer sunk. Many others died from exposure and disease.

Except for the Seminoles, the Cherokee were the last to go. In the early 1800s the Cherokee had adopted many of the ways of the whites who surrounded them. They thought that if they proved themselves to be "civilized," they would survive. They welcomed missionaries. They took up farming and trades, and became quite prosperous. They invented a remarkable written language, published a bilingual newspaper, and owned slaves. They followed the advice of the whites and over the years had given up parts of their land in sixteen separate treaties. They tried to resist white encroachment nonviolently and took their cases to court.

But despite a Supreme Court ruling that they had a right to stay on their land, the Cherokee were pressured by violence and intimidation to go. Whites who spoke out in their favor were jailed. When the Supreme Court ordered that a white missionary named Samuel Worcester be freed, the state of Georgia simply ignored the order. One local judge who consistently ruled in favor of the Cherokee was gradually stripped of his authority.

As president, Andrew Jackson refused to enforce the federal laws that should have protected the rights of the Indians and their supporters. He was a merchant, a land speculator, and one of the biggest slaveowners in Tennessee. Indian removal would mean even greater wealth and power for him and his friends.

Trail of Tears is the name given to the Cherokee removal which began in 1838, but the forced removals of other tribes were just as tragic. The Choctaw lost hundreds to pneumonia in one of the coldest winters on record. A fourth of the Cherokee and half of the Creek died from the horrors of their journeys west. Though small in numbers, the northern tribes were not spared from removal. The Sauk, Delaware, Fox, Shawnee, Miami, Huron, Ottawa, and others were also forced across the Mississippi.

In 1834, the Seminoles were told that they must

leave Florida. In return the Seminoles asked for a guarantee that if they moved west, they would have a right to the land and not be forced to move again.

Another major concern was the fate of the hundreds of blacks among them. Whites had long been irritated that the Indians gave refuge to runaway slaves. They planned to reclaim these people and their offspring when the Seminoles left. However, the Seminoles insisted that the black Seminoles be allowed to leave with them. The promises the government offered were unconvincing, and many chiefs spoke against leaving.

Although most of the Seminole leaders were against the removal treaty, a few chiefs and subchiefs were persuaded to sign. They thought they were signing an agreement to send a delegation to look over the Oklahoma lands. That was enough for the federal government to ratify the treaty and begin preparations for removal.

The Seminoles were ordered to assemble in December of 1835 to begin their migration. No one showed up. Instead, they began attacking the white settlements. During their raids, they rescued black slaves, who provided important information and joined their ranks. This was the beginning of the Second Seminole War. It was led by a young chief named Osceola. His wife, Che-cho-ter, was a fugitive slave who had been captured and returned to slavery. The principal chief among all the Seminoles was Micanopy. Jumper and Tustennuggee Emathla were among the other war chiefs.

Some congressmen, such as Henry Clay of Kentucky, opposed the Seminole War. But most others thought that the Seminoles were setting a dangerous example of resistance for other Indians, as well as posing a threat to the South's slave economy. They wanted the Seminole rebellion quickly put down.

Over the next seven years, the United States spent $20 million and 1,500 lives on a losing battle against a few thousand Seminoles and their enslaved allies. Major General Thomas Jesup called it "a negro, not an Indian war." Jackson called it a disgrace. Finally, in 1837, the Seminoles tired of the fight. They sought a truce, which the U.S. Army pretended to honor. Instead, their leaders were arrested and put in prison. In 1838, when Osceola died in prison of disease, his doctor cut off his head and kept it as a souvenir.

By 1838, most of the Seminoles were forced by hunger and exhaustion to seek a settlement. When the Seminoles worked out the Treaty of Fort Dade, their chief negotiator was Abraham, a black man who had been adviser to Chief Micanopy. All but a few of the Seminoles, red and black, were transported to Oklahoma.

One small group continued to fight, however. Wildcat and Alligator were two chiefs who had been tricked by a truce violation, but who managed to escape from jail. They went back to their people, and 300 of them continued to fight. In 1842, the United States simply gave up. These remaining Seminoles began permanent settlements in the Florida Everglades.

STRUGGLES IN THE SOUTHWEST

At the same time that the southeastern tribes were trying to hold on to their lands, the native people of the Southwest were struggling for their lands, too.

In 1836, most of what is now the southwestern United States belonged to Mexico. By then, Mexico was populated by Indians, whites of Spanish descent (*criollos*), and a "new race" of mixed ancestry and culture. When the Spanish invaded the Americas, they mixed with the Indians. Their descendants were called *mestizos*.

The mestizos also had some African blood. Mandingo traders had settled in Mexico as early as the fourteenth century. Black Moors were among the conquistadores who first came to the New World in the fifteenth and sixteenth centuries. And after the Spanish invasion, nearly 200,000 African slaves were brought to Mexico.

The Apache, the Pima, the Pueblo, the Navajo, and the Comanche were among the many Indian tribes who lived in the area controlled by Mexico. For two centuries they had resisted the Spanish soldiers and the Mexican soldiers who followed them. The Apache in particular were known as fighters who could not be subdued. The Mexican government tried to enslave or kill them. It would pay as much as $250 for an Apache scalp. Indians and mestizos made up the majority of the Mexican population, but the criollos controlled the government and the economy.

In 1821, Mexico had won a long war for independence from Spain. Texas was then a large area in Mexico that had very few people. U.S. immigrants were welcome in Texas as long as they agreed to become Catholic and to obey Mexican law. The Mexican government promised them protection from lawsuits for any debts they had incurred in the United States.

Three hundred families came, including some cotton planters who had lost their fortunes. By 1830, there were 30,000 U.S. immigrants in Texas, six times as many as the native Texans. Thousands of black slaves were brought in. There were antislavery laws in Mexico, but these laws were not enforced in Texas.

The *Anglo* immigrants brought their racial prejudices with them. They began to regard the native-born Mexicans with contempt. Despite their earlier promises, they held on to their religion, language, and customs. They refused to obey Mexican laws.

They wanted to make Texas an independent state. In 1835, Anglo rebels declared Texas "conditionally independent." They attacked the Mexican troops. Texas was officially declared independent on March 2, 1836, but the war between Texas and Mexico continued.

Nearly a decade later, Mexico agreed to recognize Texas as independent. In exchange, Mexico asked Texas to never annex itself to another nation. However, Texas was unwilling to agree to this treaty, because the U.S. government was at last considering annexation of Texas.

Texas had been trying to join the United States since 1836. Some people objected because admitting Texas would increase the number of slave states and give them more power. Some wealthy southern slave-owners didn't want to compete with Texas cotton growers. Others thought it was wrong to take Mexican land. Still others believed that the United States should remain a "white" country. They objected to the idea of native-born Mexicans becoming U.S. citizens. But despite these objections, the United States did annex Texas in 1845.

The annexation of Texas was part of a longtime

attempt by the United States to take Mexico's northern territories. One of the U.S. goals in the War of 1812 had been to clear the way for conquest of all of North America. Now President James Polk was trying to start a war with Mexico by sending troops across the Mexican border.

In the summer of 1845, journalist John O'Sullivan coined the expression *Manifest Destiny*. U.S. politicians were quick to adopt the term. Manifest Destiny was the belief that Europeans and their descendants were chosen by God to rule all of America. They believed that as the most superior race on earth, they were responsible for "civilizing" the Indians or even killing those Indians who stood in their way. They believed that European whites knew best how to make use of the land and its resources. The same reasoning was applied to the land and people of Mexico. One congressman called Mexican conquest "the destiny of the white race."

Polk lied to Congress. He claimed that Mexico had "invaded our territory and shed American blood upon the American soil." He asked that war be declared in self-defense.

A rush vote was forced through. Although many congressmen were against the idea of war with Mexico, they were not willing to vote against it. The bill was passed 174 to 14 in the House, and 40 to 2 in the Senate. Only a few antislavery congressmen voted against it. They feared that as a result of the war, slavery would be extended throughout Mexican territory.

Even some people who opposed the Mexican war did so because of racist feelings. One of them was Congressman Delano of Ohio, who was also against slavery. He was afraid that white U.S. citizens would end up mixing with Mexicans. He described them as "a sad compound of Spanish, English, Indian, and negro bloods" and "a slothful, ignorant race of beings."

Demonstrations in support of the war were held in major cities all over the nation. Many newspapers wrote editorials in which they talked about racial superiority and Manifest Destiny. Army volunteers were promised 160 acres of land after the war. Thousands of men volunteered.

Not everyone supported the war, though. Henry David Thoreau criticized it in his famous essay "Civil Disobedience." Although many churches were outspoken in their support, the Quaker, Unitarian, and Congregational churches spoke against the war. The American Anti-Slavery Society condemned it. Many organized workers opposed it because a growth in slavery would mean fewer jobs for free white laborers.

The war lasted two years, from 1846 to 1848. When Mexico signed the Treaty of Guadalupe Hidalgo in 1848, it gave up almost half its territory to the United States. For present-day Arizona, California, New Mexico, Utah, Nevada, Texas, and part of Colorado, Mexico was paid only $15 million.

The treaty gave rights of citizenship and property to the Mexicans living in these areas. Most of them, however, soon lost their property through taxes or unfair legal practices. Mexicans were often abused or killed. They were considered "foreigners," even though many of their families had lived there for generations.

U.S. troops had taken control of California early on

in the Mexican war, declaring it the "Bear Flag Republic." Spanish settlements were raided. The California Indians were told that more whites from the United States would soon be coming to take over their lands. They were warned that unless they cooperated they would be wiped out. In 1848, gold was discovered there. In 1850, California became a state.

In 1851, the Indian Bureau negotiated treaties with 119 California tribes. The Indians gave up claim to more than half of the state. In exchange, the treaties promised that the remaining 7,500,000 acres would be theirs forever. The U.S. Senate never ratified this treaty because of pressure from white politicians. However, no one ever told the Indians. They did not learn that the treaty was invalid until fifty-four years later, when the land they thought was theirs was sold from under them.

Before 1850, there were probably fewer than 500 Chinese immigrants in the United States. After the "gold rush" began, many young married men defied Chinese law and custom to seek their fortunes in California. They earned money by remining the claims abandoned by white miners and by taking on the jobs that white workers refused. White Californians regarded the Chinese as their racial inferiors, in much the same way as they did blacks and Mexicans. Because whites resented the growing numbers and growing fortunes of the Chinese, they became increasingly more hostile toward them.

In 1850, California passed one of the first of many racially discriminatory laws. The Foreign Miner's Tax was designed to drive the Mexicans out of the mines. It made foreigners pay much higher taxes than other people. Most of the money that financed the California government in the 1850s was collected in taxes from the Chinese.

Whites were also moving to California and the Mexican territories in large numbers. They again raised the debate over the balance of power between slave states and free states.

THE PUBLIC DEBATE OVER SLAVERY

Three major white groups took different positions on what should be done about the expansion of slavery into the western territories. But all of them considered blacks to be nothing more than property.

Free Soilers (members of the Free Soil party) did not want slavery to expand into the west. They wanted free white workers to be able to move into the territories without having to compete with slave labor. Most of them were also against the idea of allowing free blacks into the west.

The *Popular Sovereignty* group thought that the voters of each territory should decide for themselves. That meant that only whites would decide, because in most places even free, property-owning blacks were not allowed to vote.

The *Proslavery* group wanted slavery in all the new territories. Some southern states depended on breeding and selling slaves for their profits. They wanted the Mexican territories as their new markets. They also wanted a stronger federal fugitive slave law.

Since the early 1800s, about 100,000 slaves had escaped from the South to the free states. Slave catchers who tried to return them to slavery were often defied by local vigilance groups. Southerners wanted strong federal laws that would make it easier for escaped slaves to be returned to their masters.

The Compromise of 1850 gave something to each of these three groups. California became a free state. In New Mexico and Utah, free whites would decide for themselves about slavery. Southerners were given a new fugitive slave act. In addition, the slave-trading that had gone on in the nation's capital in the shadow of the White House was outlawed, although slavery itself was still legal in Washington, D.C. Of all these measures, the Fugitive Slave Law of 1850 was the most controversial. Under this new law, a sworn affidavit was all that was required to claim any black person from any location and kidnap that person into slavery. The captured individual had no right to a jury trial or to testify in his or her own defense.

Black people all over the United States reacted with anger and fear. Now there was no place where they would be safe. Even free blacks could be enslaved on the word of one white person. In mass public meetings, they debated what should be done. Most agreed that it would be useless to try to change the law.

Instead, they decided to resist it, by risking their own lives if necessary. For decades, northern blacks had aided fugitives. They and their white allies served as "conductors" or "stationmasters" on the *Underground Railroad*. This was a network of escape routes and hiding places for runaway slaves. Along the way they could find food, shelter, transportation, and friends as they sought freedom in the North or continued on to Canada.

Now groups such as the League of Freedom in Boston and the Liberty Association in Chicago were organized to fight against the slave catchers. In Syracuse, New York, a crowd used crowbars and a battering ram to break into the courthouse and free a slave called Jerry. In Boston, a slave named Shadrach was rescued by a group of blacks and whites who carried him out of the courtroom and into a waiting carriage. In both cases, the rescuers were placed under federal indictment. In both cases, the juries refused to convict them.

Congressman Thaddeus Stevens advised fugitives to "put themselves beyond [the law's] reach." Many of them did. Several hundred black Seminoles left Oklahoma for Mexico. Large numbers of Texas slaves also fled to Mexico.

Fifteen hundred others stayed in Texas. They joined the Comanche Indians, who were fighting against white settlers and the U.S. Army. From 1850 to 1860, between 15,000 and 20,000 fugitives left the northern states for Canada. They joined other blacks who had come from the United States decades earlier.

Most northern states had abolished slavery after the Revolutionary War, but northern blacks were not truly free. Their situation was in some ways worse than that of free blacks in the South. The rights of northern blacks varied from place to place, and whites were not bound to respect them. In many areas, blacks could live only in certain neighborhoods. Most public schools turned them away, even though they paid taxes. They could not hold certain jobs. They were excluded from land-grant bills which gave property to whites. Most states denied blacks the vote. In New York, blacks couldn't qualify to vote unless they owned $250 worth of property. And in Philadelphia, they were driven away from the Fourth of July celebrations in Independence Square.

Nearly every city had black artisans and merchants. Some of them were even quite wealthy. But the majority of blacks performed the menial jobs that whites refused. After 1830, however, poor white immigrants began to arrive in large numbers. Soon they were taking the jobs that blacks had always held. Blacks were often attacked, beaten, and driven from their homes. White mobs—and in certain cases, city officials—sometimes forced the entire black population of a city to flee.

Free blacks were considered "a dangerous and useless element" by whites. They were not welcome in the North or the South. Southerners worried about the example they set for the slaves. In some states newly freed blacks had to either leave or be returned to slavery.

Free blacks sometimes played a role in the slave revolts that slaveholders feared. Denmark Vesey was a free black man who organized a revolt in Charleston, South Carolina in 1822. The famous Nat Turner's Rebellion against Virginia slaveholders in 1831 included several free blacks.

In the North, free blacks aided fugitives, gave assistance to newly arrived blacks, and defended one another from the constant physical attacks of whites. They organized themselves to work against southern slavery as well as northern discrimination. Such organizations had existed since the late 1700s. In 1830, the first of several national black conventions was held in Philadelphia.

Around 1826, the General Coloured Association was formed in Massachusetts. It was mostly concerned with abolishing slavery. Like most of the black antislavery groups, it relied on a wide range of tactics, including force. One of its members was David Walker. In 1829 he published a pamphlet known as *Walker's Appeal*. It quickly became one of the most important antislavery documents ever written.

Walker believed in a God of justice. He believed that white racism and greed would bring God's judgment upon the nation unless whites gave up their evil ways. He urged blacks to use every possible means to take their freedom, including violence. "Kill or be killed," he said.

Special legislative sessions were called to discuss the *Appeal* in Georgia, North Carolina, and Virginia. It was outlawed in the South, but blacks and even some whites risked their lives to distribute it there. Southern mayors asked the mayor of Boston to jail Walker. Georgians offered a $1,000 reward for his death. In 1830, Walker suddenly fell dead on a street in Boston. Almost everyone believed that he had been poisoned.

In the 1820s, a Christian Protestant movement called the Second Great Awakening swept the nation. It called for Christians to remake the United States into a just society. Some whites responded by becoming *abolitionists*. They believed that slavery was an evil system that violated God's law and Jesus's commandment to love one another. They thought that slavery was one of the sins that kept the United States from its righteous destiny. The abolitionist movement was not, however, limited to Christians. Many Jews also were convinced that slavery was wrong.

By 1830, there were about fifty white abolitionist societies. They were often inspired by the black abolitionists, who continued their own organizations and national conventions. Many of the white abolitionists met in black churches. They used mass meetings, sit-ins, marches, demonstrations, and other nonviolent direct actions to publicize their cause.

In 1833, they formed a national organization, the American Anti-Slavery Society. The society's founder was William Lloyd Garrison, a former indentured servant. He started a newspaper called the *Liberator*. Four hundred of his first 450 subscribers were black. Garrison said, "I never rise before a colored audience without feeling ashamed of my race." He and other abolitionists traveled around the country, trying to persuade the "good people" of the United States to end the institution of slavery.

The most popular speakers were the black aboli-tionists, especially the former slaves. Two of the most famous were Frederick Douglass and Sojourner Truth.

As a young man, Douglass escaped from slavery in Baltimore by pretending to be a sailor. Within three years, he had become known as a powerful, eloquent speaker. Douglass could bring his audiences to laughter and tears. In 1847, he began publishing his own antislavery newspaper, the *North Star*, In time, he became the most influential of all the black aboli-tionists.

Sojourner Truth was called Isabella as a slave in upstate New York. She became free under New York law in 1927. She was a deeply religious woman. She said she was given the name "Sojourner because I was to travel up and down the land showing the people their sins and being a sign to them." When she "told the Lord I wanted another name," he "gave me Truth, because I was to declare the truth unto people." Sojourner Truth was a powerful speaker.

Abolitionist leader Frederick Douglass: "If there is no struggle there is no progress." (Courtesy of The Library of Congress)

She was widely admired for her plain speaking and strength of character. She also became well known as a champion of women's rights.

Before 1836, the American Anti-Slavery Society did not allow women to participate. Lucretia Mott was a white abolitionist and female suffragist. With seventeen other women, both black and white, she formed the Philadelphia Female Anti-Slavery Society in 1833. Female societies far outnumbered men's. Most of the money for abolitionist activities was raised by the women. The first female antislavery society was organized by black women in Salem, Massachusetts in 1832.

In 1840, the American Anti-Slavery Society split over such issues as the role of women and the appropriateness of radical action. Many blacks were soon convinced that white abolitionists were committed to ending slavery, but not racism, not even within their own organizations.

The number of abolitionists was never very large compared with the rest of the U.S. population. Most people either supported slavery or were indifferent to it. Even some people who opposed slavery hated or resented blacks. By the 1850s, many whites were openly calling for the "Indian solution" to the "Negro problem." By this, they meant that blacks who were not enslaved should be killed.

The American Colonization Society offered another plan. The society had been organized by southern whites in Congress in 1815. It called for free blacks to be shipped back to Africa, to set up colonies there.

Some blacks supported the idea of emigration. In fact, Captain Paul Cuffe, a free black activist and shipbuilder, had already taken thirty-eight people to

President Abraham Lincoln and abolitionist Sojourner Truth.
(Courtesy of The Library of Congress)

Sierra Leone in 1815. Many believed that free blacks would never be granted full citizenship in the United States. One of them was John B. Russwurm, coeditor of the first black newspaper, *Freedom's Journal*.

Most blacks were against the idea of forced massive migrations, although they supported individuals who chose to emigrate. They believed that their blood and toil had earned them the right to share in the wealth and privileges of the United States. They also thought that free blacks were needed in the United States to help others resist slavery.

Martin R. Delany agreed that blacks had a right to American soil but thought they needed a homeland in order to be "elevated" to their rightful destiny. Like most blacks, he distrusted the American Colonization Society. He believed that blacks had to make migration plans for themselves. In the 1830s, he traveled across the Appalachians in search of a suitable place, but he found racism everywhere.

By 1852, Delany had decided that the best place would be south of the United States. He urged blacks to learn Spanish in preparation. His explained his ideas in a document called *The Condition, Elevation, Emigration, and Destiny of the Colored People of the United States, Politically Considered*. In later years, he would give up on America and urge emigration to Africa.

In 1854, Congress passed the Kansas-Nebraska Act. Kansas and Nebraska were huge new territories that took up almost all the land inhabited by the Plains Indians. When these territories were opened to white settlement, the slavery question was raised again—despite the fact that the Missouri Compromise had prohibited expansion of slavery to the north. The Kansas-Nebraska Act left the decision to the white voters in the territories. For four years, open warfare was waged in Kansas between proslavery and antislavery advocates.

In 1857, the U.S. Supreme Court handed down the Dred Scott decision. Scott was a slave who had been taken to a free state by his master in the 1830s. He had also lived in territory that was free according to the Missouri Compromise. On those grounds, he sued for his freedom. The Court ruled against Scott. It said that blacks could not be citizens and had no rights that white people were bound to respect. The Court also decided that the Missouri Compromise was unconstitutional because it deprived white citizens of their right to enjoy their property.

Blacks were angry and disillusioned. Many abolitionist leaders had believed that slavery could be ended by political means. Now they realized that they had no political power. Some renewed the call for emigration, and many free blacks did leave the country.

Others called for insurrection. In 1858, John Brown led an attack against the government arsenal at Harpers Ferry, Virginia (now West Virginia). He planned to burn the arsenal and destroy the weapons there. Most of Brown's men were killed in the attempt. A young black printer named Osborne Anderson was the only one who escaped. Brown and several others were captured and hanged.

The state of Virginia insisted that Brown's raid was not important. Still, it spent $250,000 on the trial and stationed thousands of soldiers in the area. In his last speech, Brown said, "Had I so interfered in behalf of any of the rich, the powerful, the intelligent, the so-called great . . . every man in this court would have deemed it an act worthy of reward rather than punishment." Brown was feared because he was one of the few whites who were willing to fight and die to end slavery.

THE CIVIL WAR

When the Civil War began in 1861, the Union was not interested in abolishing slavery. The real issues were economic, not moral. The northern industrialists wanted free land, free labor, and high tariffs to protect their manufacturing interests. They wanted the Union to remain intact. Southern planters wanted free trade to protect their exports, and new markets for selling slaves. They feared that the proindustrial Republican party would end the expansion of slavery. They wanted states to be able to leave the Union if they chose.

In his first Inaugural Address, President Abraham Lincoln had even offered assurances to the southern states. He said, "I have no purpose, directly or indirectly, to interfere with the institution of slavery in the States where it exists." Lincoln and his advisers assumed that the southern rebellion would be put down in a matter of weeks. As it dragged on, the war became more and more unpopular in the North. Poor whites had always resented free blacks. They resented being drafted into a war over slavery even more. Riots broke out in several northern cities. Blacks were attacked and killed.

By 1862, Lincoln was anxious to end the war. He proposed amendments to the Constitution that would free the slaves by 1900, pay their former owners, and ship the freed people out of the United States.

In September he announced the Emancipation Proclamation. It said that if the Confederate states did not end their rebellion by December 31, 1862, slaves in those states would be free. He signed it into law on January 1, 1863.

The Emancipation Proclamation did not end slavery. It did not apply to Delaware, Kentucky, Maryland, Missouri, West Virginia, and parts of Louisiana and Virginia, all of which were still loyal to the Union. One million enslaved black people in those states would not be affected by the proclamation. The truth was that even in the Confederate states, the U.S. government had no power to enforce the proclamation.

Although many whites were against the draft, many blacks were eager to fight. For them, the war was about ending slavery. Northern black leaders demanded the right of blacks to enter combat. In November 1862, the attorney general declared that "free men of color, if born in the United States, are citizens of the United States." This decision opened the way for blacks to join the Union army. They were not allowed to, however, until 1863. Even then, some had to fight their way past armed white posses to enlist.

By the time Lincoln gave his approval, some generals had already recruited former slaves from the Confederate territories. Most black soldiers came from the South. Louisiana contributed the biggest number. In Tennessee and Kentucky, at least 40 percent of all eligible black men joined the Union army. Black troops fought in over 400 battles. In 1863 and 1864,

they fought in thirty-nine major battles, sometimes leading the attack. Their participation helped turn the tide of the war.

One of the most famous recruits was Harriet Tubman, who had freed herself and hundreds of others before the war. She served as a spy and led scouting raids. She was the first woman to lead U.S. Army troops in battle.

Two hundred thousand black civilians worked in the Union camps. Many of them were former slaves who had left the plantations when they heard that the Union army was near. Their labor freed up soldiers for combat.

In some areas they set up communities of their own. Blacks came from all over the South to join them. They built homes, schools, and churches. They raised crops that provided food and profit for the Union troops.

Confederate leaders also talked about using blacks in combat. One general argued, "If slaves make good soldiers, our whole theory of slavery is wrong." By the time they made up their minds, the war was over. The Confederacy probably would have regretted making the decision sooner. Blacks in Virginia had already decided to join the Confederate army if they were asked. But once they got into combat, they planned to support the Union by firing on the Confederates.

As late as 1864, Republican leaders were still not committed to abolishing slavery. There was talk of a truce with the South. They were willing to allow slavery to continue. They thought the courts should decide whether the Emancipation Proclamation and other wartime measures were legal.

Even after the war ended, black freedom was still undefined. Issues like land rights and voting rights were still being debated in Congress. Even the white leaders of the abolitionist movement were divided in their opinions.

Slavery was still legal, despite the war. The Thirteenth Amendment had been passed by Congress, but it had not yet been ratified by the states. Blacks in the "loyal" states were technically still enslaved, since the Emancipation Proclamation applied only to the Confederate states.

Black people in the slave states didn't much care that the legal issues still had to be worked out. As far as they were concerned, freedom had come. In Louisville, Kentucky 120,000 people gathered on the Fourth of July to celebrate. Soon it was clear that the war, which had started over economic conflicts, had ended up freeing four million people of African descent from slavery.

Still, the struggle for freedom was far from over.

REVIEW QUESTIONS

1. What were some of the tactics used to take possession of lands occupied by Indians? Were they legal?
2. Why was the Second Seminole War fought?
3. What did the doctrine of Manifest Destiny mean?
4. Why did the United States go to war against Mexico in 1846?
5. Who was the target of discrimination in California's Foreign Miner's Tax?
6. What four changes did the Compromise of 1850 establish? What were the two major rulings of the Dred Scott decision? How did all these events lead to the Civil War?
7. What effect did the Fugitive Slave Act and the Dred Scott decision have on black emigration?
8. Why was there tension between free blacks and white immigrants?
9. What was the "Indian solution?"
10. Was the purpose of the Civil War to end slavery?

4 | **Stemming the Tide of Freedom**

How was the law used to guarantee freedom and justice following the Civil War?
What laws and practices denied racial justice?
Who was affected by these laws?

THE IMMEDIATE POSTWAR PERIOD

After the Civil War, southern roads were filled with black people. Many of them were now searching for husbands, wives, parents, or children who had been sold away and lost to them, perhaps for years. Others were traveling out of fear that if they stayed put, their old masters would find a way to make them slaves again. Many were going to claim the land that they believed the government had promised them. But few had adequate food, clothing, or shelter, and real jobs were scarce.

During the last few days of the war, the federal government had established the Freedman's Bureau to help former slaves and white refugees. Black abolitionists like Martin Delaney were among the agents hired by the government. When they arrived in the South, they found black people already setting up schools. The bureau set up more schools and medical clinics. It distributed food and supplies.

It also seized land that had been abandoned by the Confederates and distributed it to former slaves. Some congressmen, such as Thaddeus Stevens and Charles Sumner, supported this idea. Most of their colleagues did not. Stevens wanted all the newly freed blacks and all the whites who had been loyal to the Union to receive forty acres of land. Blacks on the islands along the coasts of South Carolina, Georgia, and northern Florida actually did begin farming the land.

Even before the war was over, blacks all over the South had organized to demand their legal rights. In the farming areas, the strongest demand was for land and self-government. In the cities, blacks stressed the right to vote and participate in the political process. Everywhere, they were refusing to live by the old rules. They demanded to be treated with courtesy. They organized schools, social welfare guilds, and protective associations. They held labor strikes, "ride-ins," and marches. When they protested against unfair treatment, they were often met with white mob violence. Sometimes police led the mobs.

In most places, blacks looked to the Union army to help them. At the end of the war, it was made up mostly of black soldiers. The "Black and Blues" enforced the laws and protected the rights of the blacks. They helped the Freedman's Bureau carry out its work. They also encouraged other blacks to hold out for their own land instead of going back to work for the white planters.

Southern whites, especially the ones who had owned property before the war, resented having to treat former slaves as equals. They particularly re-

sented the presence of the black soldiers. They peti-
tioned President Andrew Johnson to remove them.

Johnson was a Tennessee slaveholder who had
become president after Lincoln was assassinated. He
was sympathetic to the former slaveowners. He said,
"This is a country for white men, and by God, so
long as I am President, it shall be a government for
white men." He had black troops removed. He ordered the Freedman's Bureau to stop redistributing
land and return it to the planters. And he appointed
provisional governors who shared his opinions about
white supremacy.

THE BLACK CODES

By the end of the year, the southern states had
enacted *Black Codes*. These laws were very much like
the old Slave Codes. They were meant to keep blacks
under control. The codes not only brutalized blacks
but also prevented them from making their own
choices about how and where they would work. Poor
whites were hired as patrollers to enforce the codes.

Some laws prohibited blacks from owning or renting property in certain areas. Most southern states
also had vagrancy laws. In many places, any black
person who refused to sign a work contract with a
white employer was considered a vagrant.

Like the property laws, vagrancy laws were intended to keep blacks from moving around in search
of new jobs or from working their own land. There
were harsh punishments for breaking work contracts.
For example, Mississippi's codes had clauses that
permitted employers to hunt down workers—just like

the old fugitive slave law. In South Carolina, vagrants could be sentenced to a year of hard labor.

Other laws controlled the kind of jobs blacks could perform. In South Carolina, any work other than farming or domestic labor required a special permit. Apprenticeship laws allowed black children to be taken away from their parents to work for white families.

The Black Codes made it legal for white "masters" to whip their black workers. They created specific punishments for blacks for such offenses as "insulting gestures." They prohibited blacks from owning military weapons. In some places, they even dictated their bedtimes.

Besides the harsh laws, blacks were victims of violence. All over the countryside, they were beaten, mutilated, and murdered. Many had their ears cut off by their former masters. In the cities, police and government officials directed mobs to attack and destroy black homes, schools, and churches. Blacks were beaten and raped. Hundreds were killed and many more wounded.

Blacks organized petitions and protests against the Black Codes. One of the most significant petitions was drawn up at the Colored People's Convention, held in 1865 near Charleston, South Carolina. In it, blacks asked Congress for "equity and justice" and offered to extend the "right hand of fellowship" to the former slavemasters in order to rebuild the South.

RECONSTRUCTION

More than anything else, it was the racist "riots" that finally moved Congress to act. In December 1865, its members honored the request of the black conventions to refuse to seat the southern congressional representatives. The following April, radical Republicans in Congress passed a civil rights bill over President Johnson's veto.

The Thirteenth Amendment had abolished slavery, but it had not mentioned citizenship for the former slaves. The Civil Rights Act of 1866 declared that blacks were to enjoy the same rights of citizenship as whites.

Led by Sumner and Stevens, Congress passed other laws that began a ten-year period of rebuilding the South. This period, which historian Lerone Bennett called "the longest stride America has ever taken" toward democracy, was called *Reconstruction*.

For most whites, the main goals of Reconstruction were restoring the southern states to the Union and reviving the southern economy. For blacks and their allies, the issue was building independent lives. They wanted to vote and enjoy political representation. They believed that they should share in the land and the wealth of their labor.

In order for the Confederate states to be readmitted to the Union, three requirements had to be met: (1) 10 percent of the 1860 voting population, all of whom were white males, had to pledge loyalty to the Union. A new constitution had to be approved that (2) abolished slavery and (3) repudiated secession. Blacks and women were excluded from the process.

The Fourteenth Amendment was ratified in 1868 and the Fifteenth Amendment in 1870. The Fourteenth Amendment guaranteed all citizens equal protection under the law. The Fifteenth Amendment protected the voting rights of black men in the South.

It also extended the vote to black men in the North. Until then, only seven "free" states had allowed them to vote.

The following year, Congress passed a series of Reconstruction acts, which placed the South under military control. New elections were authorized in which all males could vote. Under this new policy, black voters outnumbered white voters in Alabama, Florida, Louisiana, Mississippi, and South Carolina, by as much as nine to one.

Before the war, the planters had controlled the wealth and the governments of the South. In 1850, 1,000 families received nearly half of the South's income. About 660,000 families received the rest.

Of the 1,363,000 citizens who registered to vote during Reconstruction, half were white. Many poor whites were voting for the first time. Since most of them did not own property, they had not been allowed to vote under the old laws. Some poor whites recognized that the improvements blacks sought would also benefit them.

Southern white Democrats tried to control these new voters in two ways. The first was persuasion. They tried to appeal to white supremacy among the poor whites. They tried to convince blacks that the southerners had always been their friends, and that it was the North that was responsible for slavery. Few were convinced.

Their other tactic was violence. Before the war, poor whites had made up the slave patrols. After the war, the South's "leading citizens" took over. In 1867, powerful white men came from all over the South to meet at Maxwell House, Nashville's newest and biggest hotel. There, these politicians, clergy-

The racist Ku Klux Klan used rituals and terrorism in its fight
against civil rights; it is still a nationwide organization.
(Courtesy of The Library of Congress)

men, businessmen, and Confederate officers began a terrorist organization known as the Ku Klux Klan. The Klan organized violent campaigns of fear and intimidation. Its targets were blacks and their white allies.

Despite the burnings, beatings, rapes, and lynchings, all the southern states elected Republican-dominated constitutional conventions. The number of black representatives to the conventions ranged from 10 percent in Texas to 61 percent in South Carolina. Blacks played important roles in each state, especially Louisiana, South Carolina, and Mississippi.

The conventions did more than follow the requirements for rejoining the Union. They also wrote into the states' new constitutions measures that benefited white women and poor whites as well as blacks. Public education, the right of women to own property, and the right of all males to vote were some of these constitutional guarantees.

Blacks also shared power in the Reconstruction governments that followed the conventions. Nearly 800 blacks served in southern legislatures between 1869 and 1901. Their numbers were never large enough to control any of the state governments, but they did exercise considerable political power. They also filled state offices such as governor, lieutenant governor, treasurer, secretary of state, and superintendent of education. Many more served in local governments. Historian Lerone Bennett wrote, "If there was anything Southern whites feared more than bad black government, it was good black government." They had predicted that the new governments would collapse from corruption and poor management. They didn't. Instead they improved the lives of most southern citizens.

Thousands of black and white children went to school for the first time. Roads, bridges, and other structures that had been destroyed or neglected during the war were repaired. Orphanages, hospitals, prisons, and insane asylums were built. Women were legally entitled to their own wages. Anti-Semitic laws were repealed. Tax laws that had favored the wealthy landowners were changed. In some states, production went up and economies prospered.

Southern racists claimed that the Reconstruction governments were corrupt. Overall, there was probably less corruption in the Reconstruction governments than in the nation as a whole. In some states, there was less than there had been before the war. The large debts that the states accumulated during Reconstruction were not the result of corruption, as the southern racists claimed. They were mostly due to the costs of rebuilding a region destroyed by war, and to creating public services where none had existed before.

The southern racists also said that black legislators were ignorant and uneducated. In fact, ten of the twenty-two black congressmen had gone to college. Five were lawyers. Robert Elliott owned one of the largest private libraries in South Carolina. Most of the blacks had more formal education than Lincoln. Some of the most able legislators, however, such as Jeremiah Haralson, had little or no formal education.

Many of the black legislators proved to be brilliant politicians. P. B. S. Pinchback of Louisiana held more major offices than any other black in U.S. history. He served as lieutenant governor and governor. He was elected to both houses of Congress within a period of several months. Robert Elliott was twice elected to represent South Carolina in Congress. Both times he resigned to return to the state legislature, where he felt he could have more impact on the state's racist policies and practices.

Elliott was right. All over the South, blacks were leading and organizing within local governments. The Ku Klux Klan decided to concentrate on them and their white allies. Their families, homes, and jobs were threatened. They were beaten and driven off. Thousands were publicly tortured and brutally murdered, often in daylight. The Klan frequently clashed with civilian military corps of blacks and whites who were organized to defend against them.

In 1871, Congress outlawed the Klan. Martial law was declared in some states because of Klan activity. Doctors, lawyers, and other professionals were among the hundreds of Klansmen who were tried in federal courts. The Klan was officially disbanded, but white terrorist activity continued.

The Fourteenth Amendment was supposed to protect the rights of black citizens. But in 1873, the Supreme Court said that there were two kinds of citizenship, state and federal. The Court said that the Fourteenth Amendment only protected federal citizenship. Most rights, the Court said, came from state citizenship.

Under President Ulysses S. Grant, the federal government stopped enforcing the anti-Klan laws. By then, white supremacists were firmly in control of southern governments. The black militia and individual citizens were disarmed, by both legal and illegal means. Terrorism and violence kept many blacks and white Republicans out of the political process.

Wealthy white Democrats controlled the land and the money. They used economic threats to keep others from voting Republican. Those who did were refused jobs, medical treatment, or service in stores. In many instances blacks weren't allowed to vote at all. Armed patrols kept them away from the polling place, or the location of the polling place was kept secret from them. Whites voted several times in the same elections. Many came from other states to vote.

The Mississippi election of 1875 was one of the worst examples of these kinds of abuses. The governor of Mississippi asked President Grant for troops to stop the violence, but Grant refused. By then, the federal government was doing little to enforce the

Southern resistance and white abuse made Reconstruction a failure. (Courtesy of The Library of Congress)

laws. A congressional investigation found that the election was illegal, but Congress allowed it to stand.

Southern justice was no longer a popular issue in the North. Under Grant, many of the Klansmen already convicted under the anti-Klan laws were even pardoned. Within a few years, the Supreme Court overturned the anti-Klan laws. By 1880, it was estimated that 130,000 people had been killed in the South for political reasons.

The Hayes Compromise ended Reconstruction. In 1876, Republican candidate Rutherford B. Hayes won a close presidential election. But before he could take office, Congress had to certify him with an electoral vote. Southern Congressmen decided to hold up the counting of the electoral vote. Inauguration day drew closer, and the country still had no president. Many began to fear the possibility of civil disorder or even war.

The Republican party was controlled by northern industrialists. Many of them had made fortunes from the war. For example, J. P. Morgan bought 5,000 defective rifles from the army arsenal for $3.50 each. When fired, these rifles would blow off the soldiers' thumbs. Morgan sold the same rifles back to a Union general for $22 each. Others entered into contracts with the War Department to sell supplies to the government for much more than they were worth. Almost all of them made their fortunes through bribery and political deals, and at the expense of laborers, farmers, and small businessmen.

When the rich southern planters lost the free labor of the slaves, they lost their wealth. With Reconstruction, they also lost control over how the South's rich resources would be used. The northern industrialists worried that the southern trade unions and farmers would join with the planters to put the Democrats back in control. They decided that the time was right to make an alliance with the political leaders of the South.

Hayes' managers offered a deal that included federal economic aid for the South. The southern congressmen agreed to allow the count if the government would also agree to "home rule." This meant that all federal troops would be withdrawn. The white South would then be free to continue its racist policies without government interference. The deal was made on February 26, 1877, and Hayes became president.

After the Hayes Compromise, many blacks gave up on their dream of freedom and justice in the South. Thousands of them left Louisiana for Kansas and other northern states. Their movement was called the *Exodus of 1879*. It lasted for several years and spread to South Carolina and Alabama. About 50,000 blacks managed to leave. Thousands more were stopped by armed white patrols.

One reason the Republican government was so willing to abandon Reconstruction was that federal troops were quite busy elsewhere. Many of the 20,000 troops that Grant had sent to the South were in Texas patrolling the border with Mexico. Another 10,000 were used to put down labor strikes in the North. Thousands more were forcing Indians off their lands in the west.

THE FINAL CONQUEST OF INDIAN LANDS

In the 1860s, people headed West began using the Bozeman Trail, which cut through the Sioux's last great hunting ground. The Sioux, with three major divisions and many subdivisions, were the largest and most powerful of the Plains tribes. Some of the Cheyenne and the Arapaho lived with them. In 1851 the Santee Sioux had been tricked into signing away their lands in Minnesota, Iowa, and the Dakota territories. All that remained to them was a 20-mile-wide strip of land along the Minnesota River. When the army moved into the Powder River country, determined to build forts along the Bozeman Trail with or without a treaty, the Teton Sioux began to wage war.

Red Cloud, the Oglala leader of all the Tetons, refused to negotiate until all the forts along the Bozeman were abandoned. When the army finally pulled out, the Sioux set fire to the forts. A few weeks later, Red Cloud agreed to peace with the Treaty of 1868. As part of the treaty, Red Cloud demanded that Fort Laramie be the Teton Sioux trading post. In 1869, 1,000 warriors went with Red Cloud to trade and to receive the supplies that the treaty had promised. Red Cloud learned then that the treaty required the Sioux to live on reservations west of the Missouri River. He was told that next time, they would have to trade at the fort there.

Red Cloud protested to the federal government. Much to his surprise, the commissioner of Indian affairs welcomed Red Cloud to Washington. He invited him to talk to President Grant, who had commanded the Union army during the Civil War. This was the first time Indians had been invited to talk directly with the Great Father, as the whites referred to the president. Usually, they negotiated with army officers, politicians, missionaries, and traders.

Another surprise was that the commissioner, Ely

Samuel Parker, was an Indian. His real name was Donehogawa. He was from the Seneca tribe, and he had grown up on a reservation in New York. As a young man, Donehogawa had planned to be a lawyer. He was not allowed to take the bar exam, however, because only white male citizens could practice law in New York. Instead, Donehogawa became a civil engineer and supervised construction projects for the U.S. government.

During the Civil War, Donehogawa tried to volunteer his services to the Union but was told that it was a "white man's war." Finally, his old friend General Grant managed to get him into the Union army. It was Donehogawa who wrote out the terms of surrender that ended the war.

For the next four years, he traveled through Indian country settling disputes and thinking of ideas for changing the federal government's Indian policy. By then he had become a brigadier general. When Grant became president, he appointed Donehogawa as Indian commissioner.

Donehogawa began the job by replacing the corrupt officials in the Bureau of Indian Affairs (BIA). In 1849, the BIA had been transferred from the War Department to the Department of the Interior. Donehogawa set up a civilian Board of Indian Commissioners to watch over the bureau's activities. He recommended that Indians be put on this board, but none were appointed. He put a stop to many schemes to take away Indian lands and money.

Donehogawa thought that negotiations with Red Cloud might restore peace to the Plains. He sent an army escort to accompany Red Cloud and fifteen other Oglala Sioux to Washington. Without telling

Red Cloud first, he also invited Spotted Tail, chief of the Brule Sioux.

During their visit, Donehogawa won the confidence of the Sioux. He helped them negotiate a new interpretation of the treaty. It allowed them to leave the reservation and live on their hunting grounds if they wished. The Black Hills, Powder River, and Bighorn country still belonged to them, mostly because the government thought the land was worthless.

Donehogawa's reforms made him many political enemies. Shortly after Red Cloud's visit, his enemies in Congress held up approval of funds to buy supplies for the reservation Indians. They thought that this would embarrass Donehogawa. They also wanted to force the Indians to break the treaties by leaving their reservations to hunt for food. After several weeks, Donehogawa solved the problem by buying supplies on credit and having them quickly shipped to the reservations. His solution violated a few minor regulations. Soon after, his enemies charged him with fraud and mismanagement.

The attack was led by William Welsh, a part-time missionary who had served on the Board of Indian Commissioners. He had resigned in anger at Donehogawa for allowing Indians to practice their traditional religions. He sent to several Washington newspapers a letter accusing Donehogawa of "barbarism" and claimed he was unfit to be commissioner.

A congressional investigation not only cleared Donehogawa but also complimented him on preventing another Indian war. But by then, the damage to his reputation had been done. He was afraid that his enemies' racist attacks would continue and would prevent him from helping his people. In the summer of 1871, he resigned his post.

Around the same time, gold was discovered in the Black Hills. The Sioux called the hills *Paha Sapa*. They believed the Paha Sapa to be the center of the Earth, where warriors went to talk to the spirits and have visions. When white miners came into the Paha Sapa, violating the sacred ground and the Treaty of 1868, they were chased away or killed. Although the treaty said that the army would keep white men off Indian land, the prospectors kept coming and the army did nothing about it.

In 1873, the treaty was violated again by General George Custer. He was known to the Cheyenne as "Squaw Killer" Custer because of the way he had

White culture tried to make its Indian genocide look heroic.
(Courtesy of The Library of Congress)

massacred peaceful Cheyenne. His commander was General Philip Sheriden, who had said, "The only good Indians I ever saw were dead." Custer brought in a survey party for the Northern Pacific Railroad, even though the Indians had not given permission for a railroad to be built through their land.

The following year, Custer rode in again with 1,200 men. The Sioux were angered by this invasion. Many of them also became angry at Red Cloud for preventing them from attacking the soldiers. When Red Cloud saw how angry the young men were, he protested the invasion to officials in Washington.

Instead of making the prospectors and soldiers leave, the government sent a commission to buy the Paha Sapa. The Treaty of 1868 said that no more land could be sold unless three-fourths of the men agreed to it. When the delegation met with Red Cloud and the other chiefs, more than 20,000 Sioux, Cheyenne, and Arapahoe camped near the site to prevent the chiefs from accepting the government's proposal.

In frustration, the commission recommended that the government ignore the Indians' wishes. It said that the government should just decide for itself what to pay them for the Black Hills. It decided to declare the Indians to be in violation of the treaty.

The commissioners who negotiated the Treaty of 1868 had used a common trick. Since the treaty was written in English, they had simply lied to the Sioux about what it said. According to the treaty, the Indians had agreed to give up hunting and take up farming. Since they hadn't done so, the government could legally send the army to subdue them.

In 1876, the army began attacking Sioux villages. Even when they were ordered to kill only the warriors, the soldiers killed women, children, and old people, too. They also killed the horses and destroyed the villages.

More and more Indians began to leave the reservations. They joined the Indians who had decided to fight. Led by Crazy Horse and Sitting Bull (Tatanka Yotanka), they engaged in battle with army troops all that spring and summer.

In June, Custer led 600 soldiers and scouts in a surprise raid against a camp of 15,000 Indians at the Little Big Horn. The Indians were amazed at his recklessness. Custer was killed, along with almost 400 of his men. When scouts warned that more soldiers were coming, the warriors decided to break camp. The tribes all went in separate directions.

There were other battles after the Little Big Horn. Many of them were won by the Indians. In the meantime, the government took the Paha Sapa by forcing a treaty with the reservation Indians. They had to give up their weapons and horses. Without them, they could no longer hunt and had to depend on the government for food and supplies.

The warriors outside the reservations were running out of ammunition and food. In 1877, Crazy Horse surrendered to keep his people from starving and freezing to death. Instead of the "honorable peace" they promised, the soldiers arrested him. He was stabbed to death while attempting to escape from prison.

Soon after Crazy Horse's murder, the Sioux were moved to the new reservation on the Missouri River. Two hundred of them escaped to try to join Sitting Bull. Crazy Horse's parents were with them. On their way north, they buried his heart and bones somewhere near Wounded Knee Creek.

Sitting Bull had made his way to Canada. The U.S. government tried everything in its power to get Sitting Bull and his people back. The War Department even made arrangements with the Canadian government to set up a meeting between Sitting Bull and a special commission. Sitting Bull and his people refused to believe the commission's promises of peace. They told the commissioners that they would stay in Canada.

The Canadian government promised them protection, but no other help was given. After the bitter winter of 1880, Sitting Bull's followers began to return to the Sioux reservation. The original 3,000 dwindled to several hundred. The following summer, he and the last of his band surrendered. Despite the government's promise of a pardon, Sitting Bull was taken as a military prisoner.

The government thought that once Sitting Bull was imprisoned, he would be forgotten. Instead, newspaper reporters came to interview him. Other chiefs came to visit him and seek his advice. He always told them not to give up any more land. After his release from prison, the Sioux continued to treat Sitting Bull as a great chief. The government tried to ignore him and to undermine his authority, but he became more powerful than ever.

In 1885, Sitting Bull was so popular that "Buffalo Bill" Cody asked the Indian Bureau for permission to have him in his Wild West show. They finally agreed, glad to have him away from the reservation. In 1887, he returned to the Great Sioux Reservation to stop yet another land swindle attempt.

In 1890, the Sioux learned about the teachings of a Paiute medicine man named Wovoka. Many believed that he was the Messiah. He taught that in the spring, the world would be restored as it was before the white men came, and that the ghosts of the dead Indians would return. To prepare for this new world, he taught his followers that they should not fight and should do no harm to anyone. He taught them a special dance. They also learned to make special shirts that were supposed to protect them from anything, including the white soldier's bullets.

The whites called this new religion the Ghost Dance. When Sioux all over the Great Reservation began to dance, the white agents who administered the reservation became afraid and called in soldiers. They tried to stop the Ghost Dance by cutting off rations to the dancers and arresting their leaders. They were sure that Sitting Bull was behind the spread of the Ghost Dance. The head agent sent Indian police to arrest him. A large crowd of Ghost Dancers tried to stop the police, and Sitting Bull was killed. His people fled to other camps.

Some of them joined Big Foot, one of the leaders of the Ghost Dance. When he heard that Sitting Bull had been murdered, Big Foot decided to move his people to Red Cloud's reservation. On the way, they met some soldiers. The soldiers took them to an army camp on Wounded Knee Creek.

The next morning, the soldiers took all of the Sioux's weapons, even cooking knives and tent stakes. One old man tried to argue with them, and someone fired a shot.

Then the soldiers opened fire on the unarmed Sioux. Those who tried to flee were shot down by big

Hotchkiss army guns. Of the 350 Sioux there, 153 were killed and nearly as many died later from their wounds.

The Massacre at Wounded Knee marked the end of Indian freedom and the final conquest of their lands. Black Elk had been at Little Big Horn as a boy and survived Wounded Knee as a young man. Years later he said, "Something else died there in the bloody mud, and was buried in the blizzard. A people's dream died there."

— After the conquest was complete, the government continued its policy of "assimilating" the Indians. That meant that Indians should act as much like whites as possible. Indian children were sent to BIA schools to get a "white man's" education. Many were taken from their parents and put in boarding schools. In school, they were punished for using their native languages and taught that everything about Indian life was savage and inferior.

In 1887 Congress passed the Dawes Severalty Act (also called the General Allotment Act). It called for breaking up the reservation, giving parcels of land to individual Indians, and selling the rest to whites. Once the head of a family received his land, he would be granted U.S. citizenship.

Indian land had always been shared among all the members of the tribe. This practice continued after they were forced onto reservations. Most whites believed that Indians should take on their ideas about farming and individual ownership of land.

The land was not actually given to the Indians, though. Instead the BIA had to approve any plans for land use. The BIA was supposed to help the Indians become independent, prosperous farmers.

But the BIA often convinced them to lease or sell their property to white men for outrageously low prices. Whenever property was sold, the money was given to the BIA. The BIA would only give it to the Indians in small amounts. When the money was all gone, the Indians would have nothing to live on and no land, either.

Sometimes, the BIA would convince Indians to will their property to their white "friends." Many Indians who did so died under mysterious circumstances.

These and other tactics reduced many Indians to poverty and dependence on the government. Over the next fifty years, Indians lost ninety million of the 138 million acres of land they had owned in 1877.

VIOLENCE AGAINST THE CHINESE

While war, disease, and poverty were making the Indian population smaller, the Chinese population was growing. Chinese immigrants provided cheap labor. (In fact, after the Civil War, Chinese were brought to Mississippi to replace striking black farm workers.)

In the 1860s, the Transcontinental Railroad was built almost entirely by Chinese. Once it was finished, the Chinese were not welcome in the west. Violence against them increased. Politicians and labor leaders led the "Chinese Must Go" movement. There were anti-Chinese riots in San Francisco, Los Angeles, Denver, Colorado, and Rock Springs, Wyoming. Many Chinese were killed, and their property was destroyed by white mobs. The rioters were not punished, though, because Chinese could not testify against whites in court.

By 1880 there were 75,000 Chinese in California. In 1882, Congress passed the Chinese Exclusion Act. It stopped Chinese from immigrating to the United States for ten years. After it expired, Congress continued to renew the terms of the act for another fifty years.

After Chinese immigration stopped, violence against Chinese in the west continued. Many Chinese moved to other parts of the country. Others returned to China. Most of those who stayed settled in *segregated* areas known as Chinatowns. (*Segregation* is a set of laws or practices that keep people separated, usually by race.)

JIM CROW LAWS AND LYNCH LAW

Just as Chinese were segregated into Chinatowns and Indians were segregated onto reservations, so too were blacks in the South segregated after Reconstruction. The segregation laws were known as *Jim Crow laws*. These laws didn't begin in the South. The end of slavery by 1830 in the North led to Jim Crow laws there. By 1841, Massachusetts had a Jim Crow railroad car. But in the South, Jim Crow laws controlled almost everything that people did.

Jim Crow meant that blacks lived in separate neighborhoods, were treated in separate hospitals, and were buried in separate graveyards. They could not eat in the same restaurants as whites, attend the same theaters, or use the same toilets. On public transportation, blacks had to sit in separate cars or sections, when they could ride at all. Between 1881 and 1887, every southern state passed Jim Crow railroad laws.

Jim Crow meant separate waiting rooms, phone booths, school textbooks, and Bibles for swearing into court. Blacks and whites couldn't play checkers together in Birmingham, Alabama. In South Carolina, there was even a law against black and white mill workers looking out the same window.

Most of these laws were passed after 1883. That year, the Supreme Court heard five cases in which "persons of color" had not been allowed into white hotels, theaters, and railroad cars. The Court said that the Fourteenth Amendment made it illegal for states to discriminate, but not the "private citizens" who operated public transportation, accommodations, and amusements.

These laws were designed to humiliate blacks and make them feel inferior. Segregationists claimed that because of their ignorance, blacks didn't deserve any rights. Jim Crow school laws were meant to keep

blacks uneducated. Southern states spent three or four times as much on white schools as on black ones. There were few public high schools for blacks. In some places, there were no black schools at all. Without education, it would be harder for them to compete with whites for economic and political power.

In 1890, Mississippi passed laws that, in effect, legally prevented blacks form voting. A man had to own property, pay a poll tax, or be able to pass a literacy test in order to register to vote. White men who didn't meet these requirements could qualify under the *grandfather clause.* If a man's ancestors had voted before a certain date (one before Reconstruction, when blacks weren't allowed to vote), then so could he.

There was also an *understanding clause.* A man who couldn't read or write could still qualify to vote by explaining a section of the Constitution. No matter how well black men could read, write, or explain the Constitution, they never passed the literacy or understanding tests.

Worse still was *lynch law,* which wasn't really the law at all. Blacks who refused to be controlled, humiliated, and made afraid by other laws were lynched by white mobs. Others were hung, shot, cut to pieces, or burned just for sport. By the 1890s, a black man or woman was being lynched almost every other day.

Lynchings were festive family events for many southern whites. They were advertised in newspapers. Crowds came from long distances to watch or take part. Sometimes they even chartered trains. Ida B. Wells-Barnett was a journalist in Memphis, Tennessee. In 1892, three of her friends were lynched. They had angered a white grocer by opening a more successful store of their own. Wells-Barnett wrote an editorial about the incident that angered the whites even more. While she was away, her newspaper office was burned down, and she was told to never return to Memphis again.

Wells-Barnett moved to the North and began an international antilynching campaign. She used Pinkerton detectives to help her investigate every known lynching over the past decade. She found that the reasons for lynching were usually economic or political. Blacks were lynched for "crimes" such as testifying against whites, trying to vote or change jobs, or being disrespectful to whites.

Her editorials were published all over the United States. She was even invited to Britain to talk about American lynching. According to Wells-Barnett, 10,000 people were lynched between 1878 and 1898.

ACCEPTANCE OF SEGREGATION

In 1895, Booker T. Washington gave a speech that became known as the "Atlanta Compromise." In it, he advised blacks to forget about civil rights and social equality, and concentrate on learning manual skills. He assured whites that in social matters, blacks and whites could remain "as separate as the fingers."

Washington had been a slave. As a young man, he founded a black industrial college called Tuskegee Institute. He soon became the most powerful black man in the United States. Washington believed in *accommodation*, in accepting Jim Crow laws and white racism in order to make other gains. His beliefs made him popular with both northern and southern whites. Many black leaders were outraged by his views.

A year after Washington's Atlanta speech, the Supreme Court decided that racial segregation was legal. In *Plessy v. Ferguson* (1868), the Court said that the Fourteenth Amendment guaranteed political equality, not social equality or race-mixing. It said that it was reasonable for state laws to require "separate but equal" accommodations for blacks.

Justice John Marshall Harlan disagreed. He believed that segregation laws would lead to ideas of racial inferiority. "Our Constitution is color-blind," he wrote. He predicted that this decision would be as harmful to black people as the Dred Scott decision had been.

Harlan was right. *Plessy v. Ferguson* became the basis of racist southern law for the next sixty years. And overturning it became the goal of the most massive civil disobedience campaign this country had ever seen.

REVIEW QUESTIONS

1. What was Reconstruction?
2. When did widespread racial segregation begin?
3. Did the Fourteenth Amendment guarantee equal rights for Indians?
4. What were some of the legal provisions used by southern states to prevent blacks form voting? Did the same provisions apply to white men? What was the grandfather clause?

5. Which of the western Indian tribes was the most numerous and powerful? What was their most sacred place called? Why did the U.S. government try to take it away in 1876? What famous battle was the result?

6. What event is considered the last and most symbolic in the conquest of Indian lands?

7. What was the intent of the Dawes Severalty Act? What was its effect?

8. How long did the Chinese Exclusion Act remain in effect?

9. What is lynching? How many people are estimated to have been lynched between 1878 and 1898?

10. What southern practice was legalized by the *Plessy v. Ferguson* decision?

5 A New Century of Protest

Why was the turn of the century considered a low point for blacks?

How did the modern era of protest against racism begin?

How did other racial and ethnic groups fare during the first half of the twentieth century?

How did "scientific racism" lead to world war?

When the twentieth century began, things seemed hopeless for black people in the United States.

For a while, white workers had joined with blacks, but by 1899, the American Federation of Labor was openly admitting whites-only unions.

In the South, state laws had stripped away the rights that federal laws had promised after the Civil War. The number of Jim Crow laws seemed to grow by the day. Grandfather clauses had reduced black voters to only a handful.

Blacks had been driven from political office. Few were left in the state or local governments of the South. George H. White, the last of the black congressmen elected after Reconstruction, finished his second and last term in 1901.

The Fourteenth Amendment had been turned into a cruel joke. Instead of protecting the rights of blacks and other citizens, it was used to protect corporations. Between 1890 and 1910, the Supreme Court heard nineteen Fourteenth Amendment cases that dealt with black rights, and 288 that dealt with corporations.

Despite its support for Reconstruction, the Republican party had proven to be the party of big business. Its labor policies hurt workers of all races. By the end of the nineteenth century, workers and farmers were no longer political allies with blacks; they had committed to the racist, pro-slavery Democratic party.

These were "the days when hope unborn had died," as James Weldon Johnson and J. Rosamond Johnson wrote in "Lift Ev'ry Voice and Sing," the song that came to be regarded as the Black National Anthem.

BOOKER T. WASHINGTON AND THE CRITICS

All things considered, it was not surprising that whites embraced Booker T. Washington as a leader. Washington was always very careful not to offend white southerners. His speeches sometimes implied that whites were justified in their contempt of blacks. Although he advised very powerful white men on national affairs, he worked hard to appear humble in public. He had so much influence that most blacks and many whites were afraid to offend him or publicly criticize him.

Washington tried to belittle black intellectuals who disagreed with him. He claimed that their education did not prepare them "to perform any kind of useful or productive labor." He accused Ida B. Wells-Barnett and her husband of "stirring up the colored people." He referred to his black critics as "unfortunate and misguided young men."

One of those critics was William Monroe Trotter. In 1901, he began a newspaper called the *Boston Guardian*. In it, he called for total struggle against racial inequality. His editorials strongly opposed Washington and his programs.

Another Washington critic was William Edward Burghardt Du Bois. Du Bois was a brilliant young scholar and writer. He had been educated at Fisk University, at Harvard, and in Europe. He was the first urban sociologist, and the first black Ph.D to graduate from Harvard. At the turn of the century, Du Bois had been published more than any other black author in America.

Du Bois published a book of essays in 1903 entitled *The Souls of Black Folk*. In one of these essays, "Of Mr. Booker T. Washington and Others," he dared to challenge Washington as the voice of black America: "so far as Mr. Washington preaches Thrift, Patience and Industrial Training for the masses, we must hold up his hands and strive with him. . . . But so far as Mr. Washington apologizes for injustices, we must unceasingly and firmly oppose [him]."

Almost overnight, the book became a classic. Du Bois became a respected leader. Black activists, intellectuals, politicians, and businesspeople were divided into Washington supporters and Du Bois supporters.

In 1905 Du Bois and Trotter organized a secret meeting of black businessmen and professionals at Niagara Falls. The next year, they met openly at

Harpers Ferry, Virginia. Other meetings followed. The Niagara Movement, as the group was called, demanded justice and equality. They organized local chapters to carry out their program of civil protest.

By then, Washington had begun to lose some of his influence. In 1906, white politicians in Atlanta used an election campaign to stir up racial violence. Blacks were murdered by white police and white mobs. When Washington advised blacks not to fight back, even his white supporters were outraged.

The Atlanta Massacre was followed by the Springfield, Illinois Massacre in 1908. For six days, blacks were beaten and lynched by Springfield's "best citizens." Hundreds were driven from the city.

Concerned whites such as William English Walling and Mary White Ovington demanded national action. Along with Du Bois and other blacks, they put out a call for a national conference on February 12, 1909, and it was held on May 30. Three hundred people came, including Trotter and Ida B. Wells-Barnett. Some whites refused to attend because the gathering seemed too "militant." Even some who attended were uneasy about opposing Washington's philosophy.

After two days of stormy debate, the National Association for the Advancement of Colored People (NAACP) was formed. Du Bois was the only black officer. He became director of research and publicity.

For twenty-four years, Du Bois served as editor of the *Crisis*, the NAACP's official journal. In fewer than ten years, it had built up a circulation of 106,000. In addition to articles on black political thought, it showcased black art and literature. The NAACP relied on legal action and education as its primary strategy, but Du Bois used the *Crisis* to urge continued protest.

There was plenty to keep the organization busy. One of its first concerns was the continuing struggle against lynching. In 1911, the Executive Committee of the NAACP protested an unusually brutal lynching in Kentucky. A black man was taken from jail to the Opera House and tied on stage. The price of admission allowed the audience to shoot at the man's body. The location of their seats determined how many times they could shoot.

In 1913, blacks all over the country celebrated the fiftieth anniversary of the Emancipation Proclamation. That same year, many southern cities established segregated housing districts. Northern cities began to consider segregated school districts. President Woodrow Wilson declared that segregation was in the best interest of blacks and started segregating federal employees in Washington, D.C.

Before his death in 1915, even Booker T. Washington saw the need for political protest. His very last article was an attack on segregation laws.

THE BIRTH OF A NATION CAUSES RIOTS

In the year of Washington's death, filmmaker D. W. Griffith produced *The Birth of a Nation*. It was the most expensive movie that had ever been made, and Griffith used techniques that had never been used before in filmmaking. The movie was based on the best-selling book *The Clansman*, which viciously stereotyped blacks and glorified the Ku Klux Klan. Griffith arranged for a private showing of the film in the White House. After viewing it, President Wilson remarked, "It is like writing history with lightning and my only regret is that it is all so terribly true."

The Birth of a Nation gave the southern racist version of slavery, the Civil War, and Reconstruction. White slaveowners were portrayed as kind and decent. Black slaves were depicted as simple, happy servants. After the war, illiterate black brutes were shown abusing white people, raping white women, and enjoying chicken legs and whiskey in the legislature. Finally, good white southern men dressed in sheets and hoods rose up to do battle with the evil blacks. In the end, they restored white supremacy to the South.

The NAACP picketed *The Birth of a Nation* at its New York premiere. Other organizations, white and black, joined massive protest demonstrations in other cities. Riots broke out. It was eventually banned in five states and nineteen cities.

White audiences loved the film. Ad campaigns in the South promised, "it will make you hate." At the end, audiences screamed and cheered. After the film was released, the popularity of the Klan soared. In December 1915, the Klan received a charter from the Superior Court in Georgia.

THE GREAT MIGRATION AND THE FIRST WORLD WAR

During the same time, southern blacks participated in the first wave of the *Great Migration*. Between 1910 and 1920, 300,000 left the rural South for Chicago, New York, Detroit, and other northern cities. In the next decade, another 1.3 million came. By the end of the Second World War, more than five million had moved North.

As northern black populations increased, the politics and economies of the cities changed. In the South, the majority of blacks had worked in agriculture. In the North, most worked in service jobs. After the migration, more blacks began to work in manufacturing and industrial jobs. They began their own businesses and insurance companies. They demanded civil and political rights. They elected blacks to public offices.

The first wave of the Great Migration coincided with the First World War. More than 370,000 black soldiers and 1,400 commissioned officers served in the war. About half of them went to France.

There was very little racial segregation in France. White Americans worried about race-mixing there. French officers were ordered not to socialize with black officers. Blacks were described to them as "a constant menace to the American who has to repress them sternly." They were advised to prevent intimacy between black men and white Frenchwomen to keep from " 'spoiling' the Negroes."

All during the war, blacks in the United States were under attack. In 1917, one of the worst race riots in history occurred in East St. Louis, Illinois. White mobs killed between forty and 200 blacks, and drove 6,000 from their homes.

In 1918 and 1919, the number of lynchings rose. In Valdosta, Georgia, a pregnant black woman named Mary Turner was hanged and set afire. Her abdomen was ripped open with a pocketknife. The unborn baby was stomped to death.

Blacks protested these brutal acts in marches, speeches, and newspaper articles. Government officials tried their best to halt the protests.

Labor leader Asa Philip Randolph was arrested after one of his speeches. In New York, FBI agents stormed the NAACP offices to question Du Bois. The next issue of the *Crisis* was held up for twenty-four hours by postal authorities. President Wilson thought about having black editors and leaders arrested but changed his mind.

RACIAL VIOLENCE AFTER THE WAR

In 1919, black soldiers left the war in Europe and came home to race wars in the United States. During the "Red Summer" of 1919, race riots broke out in twenty-six different U.S. cities. In some places, such as Chicago, the fighting lasted as long as thirteen days.

In the 1920s, the Klan began to spread to the North. Hundreds of thousands of whites were recruited in the Midwest. In Oklahoma, Klan violence was so bad that martial law was declared. By 1924, the Klan had at least four million members. Most of them were poor white men from rural areas.

In the face of such racial violence, many black people gave up on the idea of interracial unity. During the war, Marcus Moziah Garvey, a Jamaican immigrant, began an organization called the Universal Negro Improvement Association. Garvey believed "that the white race should uphold its racial pride and . . . the black race should do likewise." His slogan was "Africa for Africans at home and abroad."

Millions of blacks heard his message. Poor and working-class blacks especially supported his ideas. In a two-year period, Garvey received $10 million in contributions. He organized restaurants, stores, laundries, hotels, factories, and a steamship company called the Black Star Line. In 1923, he declared himself the provisional president of Africa. In 1925, Garvey was convicted of mail fraud and sent to prison. He was pardoned by President Calvin Coolidge and deported to Jamaica in 1927.

THE NATIVIST MOVEMENT

While Garvey was advising blacks to emigrate from the United States, *nativist* sentiment was making it nearly impossible for anyone except northern Europeans to immigrate into the United States. Nativism began in the 1700s as a movement to protect the interests of native-born Americans against foreign immigrants. In the 1800s and early 1900s, it was applied to specific groups. Intellectuals offered "scientific" evidence that the white "races" of southern and eastern Europe were inferior to northern European "Teutonics." The same evidence was the basis for Nazi racism later in the twentieth century.

In the early 1920s, nativists succeeded in passing laws that required literacy tests and head taxes for immigrants. In 1921, the Johnson Act set up severe restrictions on the number of European immigrants.

In 1924, the Johnson-Reed Act set up immigration quotas that favored northern Europeans and limited eastern and southern Europeans to very small numbers. The number of Africans and Asians allowed to immigrate was even tinier, and Japanese immigration came to a complete halt. The same year, Congress established the Border Patrol to keep Mexicans out.

Nativist sentiment was one reason for the tremendous growth of the Klan in the 1920s. The Klan was not only antiblack, but also antiforeigner. Jews and Catholics were among the Klan's particular targets.

Blacks, Mexicans, Asians, and eastern and southern Europeans were treated as second-class citizens. Until 1924, Indians were not citizens of the United States at all. The Snyder Act changed that for the worse. "In recognition of services rendered" during the war, all Indians became citizens. Now they had to pay taxes, and many Indians lost their land to local governments. This change in policy did not necessarily mean that Indians were allowed to hold public office or to vote in state and local elections. It did mean that Indians could now be drafted into the military, whether they wanted to serve or not.

ROOSEVELT AND THE NEW DEAL

In 1929, Chicago voters elected Oscar DePriest to Congress. He was the first black congressman since 1901. By then, there were large numbers of black voters in several northern cities. The next year, black voters prevented the Senate from confirming Judge John H. Parker as a Supreme Court justice. Parker had once opposed giving blacks the vote. This campaign was called "the first national demonstration of the Negro's power since Reconstruction days."

Until the end of Reconstruction, blacks had always thought of the Republican party as a friend. Even after the party betrayed black hopes by dismantling Reconstruction, many had remained loyal. But during the Depression, huge numbers of blacks voted for Franklin D. Roosevelt and his "New Deal" policies.

During his speeches and press conferences, Roosevelt began to talk about the problems that blacks faced. Instead of mentioning any group by name, he spoke of the "underprivileged." His New Deal policies focused on economic problems. But an international scandal that began in the early 1930s and continued throughout Roosevelt's administration demonstrated the problems of racial injustice in the legal system.

In Scottsboro, Alabama, in 1931, nine black youths were accused of raping two young white women. One of the women was a known prostitute, and the other woman later changed her story. There was little or no evidence that there had been a rape. Still, eight of the nine youths were convicted and sentenced to die.

In 1932, the Supreme Court overturned the Scottsboro convictions because the youths had not had legal counsel. They were tried and convicted a second time. The Court again set aside the convictions because blacks had been excluded from the jury. In 1937 charges were dropped against five of the Scottsboro defendants. The other four were tried and convicted a third time. Three of them had been paroled by 1950. The fourth escaped and later died in prison.

Most people believed that Roosevelt opposed racial discrimination. Early in his administration, he established a group of advisers known as the Black Cabinet. It included educators, lawyers, economists, and other professionals. One of Roosevelt's best-known black advisers was Mary McLeod Bethune, who founded Bethune-Cookman College in Daytona Beach, Florida. His most influential adviser, however, was his wife, Eleanor Roosevelt. Much of the credit for Roosevelt's progressive policies is owed to Mrs. Roosevelt.

The New Deal helped people all over the United States, but it helped blacks the most because they had been hit hardest by the Depression. New Deal projects created better housing and schools. Its programs allowed people to purchase land, own homes, and have electricity. It established minimum wages and set maximum hours for workers. Over one million black people found jobs through New Deal agencies.

The New Deal era also brought a change in federal Indian policies. The Wheeler-Howard Act of 1934 helped restore tribal lands and tribal governments. But the Bureau of Indian Affairs still maintained control over the tribal governments' decisions.

For many Indians, the New Deal turned out to be a bad deal. For instance, Navajo herders were forced to destroy 40 percent of their cattle, sheep, and goats. The government's plan was to move the Navajo from herding to farming. But the irrigation projects that would make farming possible were not completed because Congress did not approve the funds. With their flocks and herds gone, the Navajo went hungry. In a few years, they went from being self-supporting to depending on government handouts.

Racism and discrimination existed within all the New Deal programs. Construction projects that used public funds were supposed to hire a certain number of black workers. They often didn't. Payments that were supposed to go to sharecroppers often ended up in the landowner's pockets. There were many other problems as well. However, the New Deal programs did help many people survive and focused the nation's attention on the problems faced by blacks and other poor people.

THE PERSISTENCE OF BLACK UNEMPLOYMENT AND SEGREGATION

Even with the New Deal, black unemployment was high. In several cities, campaigns were organized to boycott stores that hired only white workers, even though most of their customers were black. In New York, the campaign created 10,000 jobs.

The American Federation of Labor (AFL) talked about equal opportunity but did nothing to help most workers. Blacks were still barred from most AFL unions, along with women, foreigners, and unskilled laborers. Asa Philip Randolph tried to force the AFL to recognize black workers. Randolph was the leader of the 35,000-member Brotherhood of Sleeping Car Porters. In 1934, he convinced the AFL to organize a Committee of Five.

The committee was supposed to give a report on the condition of black workers at the 1935 AFL convention. Its report recommended that the unions stop barring blacks from membership, give them representation at conventions, and end Jim Crow local unions. However, the report was never given, and the AFL resisted change. The same year, a new group called the Congress of Industrial Unions (CIO) was formed. The CIO encouraged blacks to join.

When World War II began, many new jobs were created in defense plants. Even though there was a shortage of labor, most plants refused to hire blacks. Others would hire them only as janitors, even if they had other skills. Even government training programs

Although they fought in every war, black soldiers came home as second-class citizens. Many joined the struggle for civil rights.
(Courtesy of The Library of Congress)

excluded blacks. In the armed forces, blacks were segregated in some branches and excluded entirely from others.

By then organizations such as the NAACP and the Urban League were strong. Demonstrations, protests, and petitions called for fair practices in government, industry, and the military. In 1941, Randolph organized a march that would bring 100,000 people to Washington. To stop the march, President Roosevelt issued an executive order that banned discrimination in war industries and government training programs. But it did not mention discrimination in the armed forces.

The army remained segregated by units. Blacks were not allowed to serve in the air corps or the marines. By the end of 1941, the army had opened a flying school in Tuskegee, Alabama, to train black pilots, but they served in segregated squadrons. In the navy, they could only serve as messmen. Many of them felt bitter about fighting a war for rights that would be denied to them. The United States condemned Nazi atrocities against Jews and the bombing of Chinese civilians, but continued to practice violence and discrimination against Jews and Chinese in the United States. One black soldier said, "Just carve on my tombstone, 'Here lies a black man killed fighting a yellow man for the protection of a white man.' "

Even blood was segregated. In the Red Cross blood banks, blood was separated by the donor's race. Dr. Charles Drew, a black physician and scientist who developed the blood bank system, was put in charge of the wartime donations project. He was forced to resign when he tried to stop this practice.

Dr. Drew later died in an automobile accident in

North Carolina. At that time blacks were not admitted to white hospitals in the South. Many people believe that Drew died because he was denied a blood transfusion at the white hospital where he was first taken.

The Congress of Racial Equality (CORE) was formed in 1942 by a group of black students from the University of Chicago. While the NAACP attacked segregation in the courts, these young people decided to begin nonviolent, direct action. After a Chicago restaurant refused to serve them coffee, they organized a successful sit-in. More chapters of CORE were formed on other northern college campuses. By 1950, CORE actions had persuaded many restaurants, hotels, and other public facilities to serve or admit blacks.

DISCRIMINATION AGAINST MEXICANS AND JAPANESE AMERICANS

Racial discrimination was not limited to blacks. In the Southwest, signs in restaurant windows sometimes read "No Dogs or Mexicans Allowed." White newspapers often gave biased or false reports that stirred up racist fears against Mexicans. In 1943, anti-Mexican riots began in Los Angeles, California and spread to other cities across the country. These were known as the "Zoot-Suit Riots," because of a popular style of clothing worn by many young Mexican-American men.

On June 3, 1943, eleven sailors claimed that a group of Mexican boys had attacked them. The Los Angeles police raided the neighborhood, but did not make any arrests. The next night, 200 sailors began beating Mexican American youths. The police did nothing to stop the sailors, but did arrest the victims. On June 7, hundreds of whites went out into the streets looking for Mexican Americans, many of whom were beaten and stripped of their clothing. The attacks were stopped late that night by military authorities.

On the Pacific Coast, World War II renewed old anti-Asian feelings. After the Japanese attack on Pearl Harbor, President Roosevelt issued Executive Order No. 9066. It authorized the military to remove Japanese Americans from their homes and place them in federal concentration camps, known as internment camps.

Many whites argued that all Japanese Americans were still loyal to Japan. Rumors had spread that they were helping to plan an attack on the Pacific Coast of the United States. In fact, not a single case of sabotage involving Japanese Americans was ever discovered. The Japanese were interned not because they were security risks but because they were successful.

Before the war, Japanese immigrants had dominated California truck farming. Despite laws that denied them citizenship, prevented them from leasing land, and attempted to put them in segregated "Oriental" schools, many Japanese owned their own farms, fishing boats, and other businesses. When the Japanese were herded off to camps, their property and possessions were seized or sold at ridiculously low prices.

Once in the camps, the Japanese were required to fill out loyalty oaths. These forms asked if they would be willing to serve in the U.S. armed forces and if they would swear loyalty to the United States. Many Japanese Americans were afraid that if they answered "yes" to these questions, they would be drafted into the army, and that if they answered "no," they would be deported to Japan. Many of them refused to answer the questions at all. They also resisted with strikes, petitions, mass meetings, and riots against the camp authorities.

Some Japanese did try to prove their loyalty by serving in the military. Some volunteered and others were drafted. The 442nd Regimental Combat Team was made up entirely of Japanese Americans. It was the most decorated American unit in the war.

In 1944, the Supreme Court ruled that loyal citizens could not be held in the camps against their will. But the military order that had forced the Japanese into camps was never declared illegal. Justice Robert Jackson disagreed with the other justices; he felt that internment was unconstitutional. In his dissent he said that the order "validated the principle of racial discrimination." The last internment camp was not closed until 1946.

RELATIONS WITH CUBANS, FILIPINOS, AND PUERTO RICANS

When the Spanish-American War began in 1898, many people believed that the United States was helping Cuba free itself from Spain. Instead, the United States wanted to control the Caribbean. The idea of Manifest Destiny also meant taking responsibility—by force, if necessary—for the "little brown brothers" in surrounding nations. U.S. businesses wanted more cheap labor, and more markets in which to sell their goods.

The government was also afraid that the Cuban rebels might win without help from the United

States. Many Cubans, including the leaders of the rebellion, were dark-skinned people. (A few years earlier, a Florida politician had proposed that the United States buy Cuba from Spain and send American blacks there.) If they won, Cuba might become "another black republic" like Haiti. By entering the war on the rebel side, the United States could take over the government of Cuba. Thousands of American blacks fought in the Spanish-American War. But some black leaders condemned the war as hypocritical. They pointed out that the men who made up the Cuban army would face segregation and discrimination if they lived in the United States.

When the war ended, Spain "gave" Cuba, the Philippines, Guam, and Puerto Rico to the United States, even though Puerto Rico had become independent in 1897. (At the same time, Hawaii was annexed by the United States.) In 1899, the Filipino people rebelled against U.S. rule. The rebellion was put down ruthlessly by the U.S. Army. Unarmed men, women, elders, and children were slaughtered. One senator reminded his colleagues that "we are not dealing with Americans or Europeans. We are dealing with Orientals." The Filipinos were often called "niggers." At the same time, lynchings and violent attacks against people of color in the United States were increasing.

Four black regiments were sent to the Philippines. Some black soldiers wrote letters to family, friends, and newspapers about the war's racism. Others deserted to join the rebel army.

After the Filipino rebellion was crushed, the Philippines became America's best source for cheap labor. Chinese and Japanese laborers were no longer available because of immigration laws. Large numbers of Filipinos were brought to Hawaii and California as migrant farm workers.

In the 1920s, Filipinos faced the same kind of anti-Asian racism that the Japanese and Chinese had faced. However, they could not be excluded under the immigration laws because they were not aliens.

In 1934, The Tydings-McDuffie Act was passed. It promised independence for the Philippines. It also allowed only fifty Filipinos to come to the United States each year. In 1935, the Repatriation Act offered Filipinos free transportation back to the Philippines. The catch was that they could never return to the United States. The Repatriation Act did not succeed in getting very many Filipinos to leave. In the 1940s, American citizenship was extended to Filipino immigrants, and today the highest concentration of Filipinos in the United States are still in Hawaii and California.

After the First World War, migration from Puerto Rico to the United States began to increase. By 1947, more than 100,000 Puerto Ricans were migrating each year. Most Puerto Ricans settled in New York City. Their attitudes about race were very different from those of most Americans. In Puerto Rico, racial segregation had never been part of the law, and color was determined by how a person looked; in the United States, race was inherited. In Puerto Rico, there were many racial categories; in the United States, people were either black or white.

Puerto Ricans coming to the United States are not considered immigrants, because they are U.S. citizens, and are thus considered migrants. After the United States took control of Puerto Rico in the Spanish-American War, many Puerto Ricans demanded independence for their island. Instead, the Jones Act of 1917 imposed American citizenship on them. It also obligated them to serve in the U.S. armed forces. Until 1947, Puerto Rico's governors were appointed by the U.S. president. Today, the debate continues over whether Puerto Rico should remain a commonwealth, become a state, or become independent.

WHAT IS ANTI-SEMITISM?

During World War II, Nazi Germany murdered six million eastern European Jews in the name of racial supremacy. Hitler and his followers believed that the "master race" was "Nordic" or "Aryan." Their attempt to systematically wipe out Jews and several million other "inferior" people is known as the _Holocaust_.

Discrimination against Jews is called _anti-Semitism_. The Holocaust was anti-Semitism in its most extreme form. But discrimination against Jews in housing, jobs, public accommodations, and social interactions is anti-Semitism, too. Anti-Semitism, like racism, is a special kind of discrimination based on prejudices and negative stereotypes.

Is anti-Semitism racism? Not always. For hundreds of years, the Christian countries of Europe discriminated against Jews based on religion and ethnicity. Jews were considered to be white until the early 1800s, when Europeans had become very concerned about race. Jews were then classified as a dark—and inferior—race.

In the United States, Jews are generally regarded as white. When people call themselves Jewish, they may be talking about their religion, culture, or politics. When people discriminate against Jews, they may be basing their actions on any, all, or none of those factors.

REVIEW QUESTIONS

1. Who were the two most widely recognized black leaders in the early 1900s? What were their opposing viewpoints?
2. Why did a group of black business and professional men meet secretly at Niagara Falls in 1905?
3. What was the NAACP's primary strategy?
4. Why was the *The Birth of a Nation* denounced by the NAACP?
5. Why was the summer of 1919 called the "Red Summer?"
6. Where did more than five million blacks move to between 1910 and the end of the Second World War? Why?
7. What was the nativism movement? In what way did it foreshadow Nazism?
8. How did the black labor movement challenge racial discrimination? Who was the movement's spokesperson?
9. By the start of World War II, were the United States armed forces integrated?
10. What happened to many U.S. citizens of Japanese descent during World War II?

6 | The Second Reconstruction

How was the legal system used to attack institutional racism?
What form did black protest take in the 1950s?
What were the major organizations of the civil rights movement?

SEGREGATION AND MOB VIOLENCE CONTINUE THROUGHOUT THE 1940s

After World War II, segregation was still very much a fact of life in the United States.

The Brooklyn Dodgers made baseball history by signing a black man, Jackie Robinson. Kenny Washington and three other blacks were signed to white football teams. But for the most part, blacks and whites played on separate professional teams, in segregated leagues.

In Hollywood and on Broadway, talented black actors performed in all-black shows. Otherwise, the only roles open to them were usually negative racial stereotypes. Entertainers could not be served in many of the places where they performed.

Laws that segregated neighborhoods had been struck down by the Supreme Court in 1917. They were replaced by "gentlemen's agreements" that kept individuals from renting or selling to blacks in white neighborhoods. Because the neighborhoods were segregated, the schools were, too.

Segregated schools were separate, but they were far from equal. South Carolina spent $179 a year to educate white students, and only $43 on blacks. Often, black students were not taught the same subjects as white students. Instead, they learned skills that would make them better farmers or servants.

Some southern states did not allow blacks to vote in the Democratic primary elections.

In parts of the North and most of the South, white restaurants, hotels, barber shops, and other facilities refused to serve blacks. All over the South, blacks had to use separate restrooms, water fountains, and entrances. In Birmingham, Alabama, white U.S. Senator Glenn Taylor was arrested for trying to go through a door marked "For Negroes."

And along with segregation, white mob violence continued.

An NAACP report called 1946 "one of the grimmest years" in its history. It told of horrible attacks in which black veterans were blowtorched or had their eyes gouged out. It accused the nation of not living up to its wartime promises of democracy for all citizens. Later, the NAACP asked the United Nations for help.

President Harry Truman appointed a Committee on Civil Rights in December 1946. It found three reasons for ending racial discrimination in the United States: because it was immoral for a country that claimed to believe in equality; because it cost a lot to maintain "separate but equal" facilities; and because the rest of the world would have a poor opinion of the United States. President Truman took the committee's recommendations to Congress in 1948, but Congress refused to act.

Some people did not believe that Truman was sincere, because he did not use all the powers he already had. For instance, he asked Congress to outlaw segregated buses and trains that traveled between states. Such a law had already been passed in 1887 but had never been enforced.

In the late 1940s a group of black and white students from CORE and the Fellowship of Reconciliation (FOR) had tried a sit-in on segregated interstate buses. Some of them were arrested in North Carolina and sent to prison. This was the first Freedom Ride of the twentieth century.

THE NAACP WINS LEGAL BATTLES

In 1950, the NAACP decided to change its legal strategy. Until then, it had attacked segregation laws that provided unequal schools for blacks. It even had some successes in getting blacks admitted to white graduate schools where no black ones existed.

Now the NAACP decided to challenge the Supreme Court's *Plessy v. Ferguson* decision which made "separate but equal" legal. The NAACP believed that it was unconstitutional under the Fourteenth Amendment. In case that didn't work, the organization also decided to argue that integration was the only way to make schools equal. Segregation existed because whites thought that blacks were inferior. Segregated schools made black children believe that they were inferior. As long as schools were separate for that reason, no matter how good they were, they could never be equal.

NAACP lawyers traveled all over the United States looking for cases they could use. When they lost them in the state courts, they appealed to higher courts.

In 1952, the Supreme Court agreed to hear *Brown v. Board of Education of Topeka, Kansas* along with four other cases involving black schoolchildren. On the day of the hearing, hundreds of people packed the courtroom and the hallways outside. For three days, the lawyers for both sides argued their cases.

Nine months later, the Court still had not made a decision. Then, suddenly, Chief Justice Frederick Vinson died of a heart attack. Earl Warren was appointed to replace him.

The NAACP lawyers were skeptical about Warren. Even though he said he believed in equality, he had supported Japanese internment during the war. In the end, Warren decided that segregation in schools must end. In 1954, the Court announced its decision: "We conclude that in the field of public education the doctrine of 'separate but equal' has no place. Separate educational facilities are inherently unequal."

The Court's ruling applied only to public education. What was important about the decision, though, was that it did declare "separate but equal" unconstitutional under the Fourteenth Amendment.

The Court did not explain how its orders were to be carried out. Even though the final decision was unanimous, Justice Stanley Reed had not wanted to vote with the rest of the Court. He finally agreed, on the condition that school segregation would end gradually.

In 1955, the Court gave its decision on how the schools were to desegregate. Instead of giving them a definite amount of time, it said that school districts would need time to work out their problems. It ordered them to begin admitting black children to white schools "with all deliberate speed" and "at the earliest possible date." The lower federal courts were put in charge of desegregation.

Black people were angry and disappointed. After the Court had ruled so strongly against segregation, they had expected it to take a much stronger position on ending it. Now they were afraid that nothing would change.

White southerners were angry, too, but for a different reason. "Black Monday" was what they called the day the Supreme Court decided *Brown v. Board of Education.*

WHITE RESISTANCE TO INTEGRATION

In Mississippi, whites attempted to resist integration by forming the first Citizens' Council. Before long, Citizens' Councils spread across the South. These councils were known as the "white-collar Klan." Whereas the Klan was made up of mostly poor white men, who hid behind white hoods while they burned crosses or beat and murdered their victims, the Citizens' Councils were made up of urban, middle-class whites. Instead of violence, they tried to control people by threatening their jobs, cutting off their credit in stores, or refusing them bank loans. Thousands of dollars in tax money went to support the Citizens' Councils.

The leader of the white resistance was a Mississippi

judge named Tom Brady. To Brady and many other whites, integration meant race-mixing. He wrote: "The loveliest and purest of God's creatures, the nearest thing to an angelic being . . . is a well-bred, cultured Southern white woman or her blue-eyed, golden-haired little girl."

Both the Klan and Citizens' Councils vowed to resist integration. In 1955, a wave of violence began in Mississippi that was unusual even for that state. First, two NAACP organizers were lynched. They had refused to take their names off the voter registration list, and they tried to get other blacks to register. Blacks outnumbered whites in some counties. Segregationists were afraid of the power blacks would have if they voted.

The third person lynched in Mississippi that year was Emmett Till, a fourteen-year-old from Chicago. In those days, black men could be beaten and jailed, or even murdered, for the crime of "reckless eyeballing" of white women. Till was kidnapped and tortured because he said "Bye, Baby" to a white woman in a store. His mutilated body was found in a river three days later. People all over the United States were outraged by the murder. After pictures of Till's body appeared in the black press, contributions began pouring in to the NAACP.

Two white men were arrested. At their trial, Till's uncle pointed them out as the ones who had taken his nephew. It was very rare—and dangerous—for a black man to testify in court against whites, especially in a murder trial. After he spoke, another black man and his aunt testified to seeing and hearing the murder. An all-white, all-male jury found the two men "not guilty."

The nation was stunned by the verdict. For many blacks, it was the last straw. The NAACP had depended on legal action, political pressure, and public education to end segregation. Now many people felt that it was time for more direct protest actions.

NONVIOLENT PROTESTS RESULT IN STRONGER CIVIL RIGHTS LAWS

In Montgomery, Alabama, a woman named Rosa Parks was arrested because she refused to give up her seat on a bus to a white man. The black people of Montgomery organized a boycott of the buses. They demanded that the bus drivers treat them with courtesy, and that black drivers be hired. They also wanted to be seated on a first-come, first-served basis. Martin Luther King, Jr., the young pastor of the Dexter Avenue Baptist Church, was chosen to lead the boycott.

Every day 52,000 people rode the Montgomery buses. Forty thousand of them were black. When blacks stopped riding them, the bus line lost most of its customers. The downtown stores also lost business. The boycott was effective because it cost white businesses money.

The boycott leaders were arrested. Their homes were bombed. Their churches were attacked. But in the end, the segregated buses were outlawed.

Virginia Durr was a white woman who supported the boycott. When she heard the news, she "felt pure, unadulterated joy. Of course the blacks felt that way, but the white friends I had felt the way I did. We felt joy and release. It was as if a great burden had fallen off us."

Blacks in other southern cities organized successful boycotts, too. In 1957, ministers from eleven southern states met in Atlanta. They formed the Southern Christian Leadership Conference. The ministers planned to use the churches to continue the work that the NAACP had begun. They agreed that boycotts and nonviolent protests were their strongest weapons.

This was the beginning of the second Reconstruction. In August 1957 Congress passed a Civil Rights Act. It created a Civil Rights Commission. It gave the Justice Department new powers to work against voting rights abuses. The act was the first civil rights legislation since 1875.

In September 1957, President Dwight Eisenhower sent federal troops to Little Rock, Arkansas. Their job was to escort nine black children into the all-white Central High School. A few weeks earlier, Governor Orval Faubus had called out the National Guard to keep the children out. When the National Guard left, white mobs surrounded the school. The children had to have bodyguards to get in. The troops remained at Central High School for the rest of the year.

The next year, Governor Faubus closed the Little Rock public schools. Most of the white students went to private schools or schools outside the city. Most of the black students didn't go to school at all that year. In 1959, the Supreme Court ordered that the public schools be reopened and integrated.

Other southern school districts tried the same tactic. In Prince Edward County, Virginia, public schools were closed down for four years before the Supreme Court ordered them to reopen. White students in the county attended a "private" school that was sup-

Official segregation ended decades ago; de facto segregation still exists. (Copyright Washington Post; *reprinted by permission of the D.C. Public Library)*

Alabama's governor George Wallace defied the federal government's order that state universities be integrated. He was eventually defeated. (Courtesy of The Library of Congress)

ported by public funds. Most schools, however, simply ignored the integration laws.

Meanwhile, blacks were testing other segregation laws. Protests spread to cities all over the South. Organizations such as the NAACP wanted to promote civil rights legislation. But young people, in the South and the North, wanted to continue direct action. In 1960 they organized the Student Nonviolent Coordinating Committee (SNCC, pronounced "snick").

There were sit-ins at lunch counters. There were stand-ins at movie theaters. There were sleep-ins in hotel lobbies. The students were attacked, beaten, and jailed, but their demonstrations forced public facilities in 112 cities to begin serving and admitting blacks.

The 1960 presidential race between John Kennedy and Richard Nixon was very close. Neither candidate said anything about the civil rights movement. Many blacks favored Republican candidate Nixon, because Democrats controlled the segregated South.

But when Martin Luther King, Jr. was arrested during a sit-in in Atlanta, Kennedy called King's wife, Coretta, to offer his help. Kennedy's aides called the mayor and a judge in Atlanta to ask for their help. Nixon did not make any public statement about King. After the news about Kennedy appeared in the press, black voters switched to Kennedy. He narrowly won the election, thanks to the black vote.

The sit-in movement also spread to the North. Even though segregation was not required by law there, many northern cities were just as segregated as southern ones. Protests were staged in Massachusetts, Illinois, New York, and New Jersey.

The Civil Rights Act of 1960 was passed to help stop the arrests of protesters and the violence against them. It required that voting records in federal elections be kept for a certain amount of time. It gave the courts power to appoint voting referees to make sure that elections were fair, and it gave the Justice Department the power to act if a voter was discriminated against.

In 1961, CORE began to organize more Freedom Rides. Black and white Freedom Riders would board segregated buses. Blacks would sit in front of the buses, the part reserved for whites. Whites would sit in the back. At the rest stops, blacks would go into whites-only waiting rooms and try to use the restrooms and lunch counters. One group was fire bombed. In Birmingham, Alabama, another group was attacked by a mob. Some of the Freedom Riders had to be hospitalized. One of them was paralyzed for life.

But the Freedom Rides did not end. In May, another group rode to Montgomery, Alabama. They were attacked and beaten by the mob. So was President Kennedy's aide, John Seigenthaler, a white man from Tennessee. Kennedy sent 600 federal marshals to Montgomery. The next day, the governor declared martial law and sent in the National Guard.

Riots broke out at the University of Mississippi when James Meredith, a black man, enrolled there. President Kennedy went on television to ask Mississippi citizens to obey the law. Over 12,000 federal troops, marshals, and the National Guard were sent there.

One of the most important civil rights campaigns took place in Birmingham, Alabama in 1963. Birmingham was considered one of the most racist cities in the South. Its nickname was Bombingham because of the many unsolved bombings in black neighborhoods. In 1962, it closed its parks, pools, playgrounds, and golf courses rather than opening them to blacks.

Martin Luther King, Jr. was one of 2,000 people arrested in Birmingham. While he was in jail, some white ministers from Birmingham took out a full-page newspaper ad that called him a troublemaker. Using the edges of the newspaper and scraps of toilet paper, King wrote back to them. His "Letter from a Birmingham Jail" became one of the most famous civil rights documents.

After his release, schoolchildren were organized to march. They were met by police dogs. Firemen turned hoses on them that were strong enough to rip the bark off trees. It was the television pictures of children being bitten and rolled down the street by fire hoses that made the nation angry and gave the civil rights movement national support.

On August 28, 1963, more than 250,000 people came to the March on Washington. It was the largest civil rights demonstration in history. They demanded passage of a strong civil rights bill that was then in Congress. They wanted schools to be integrated by the end of the year. They asked for a fair employment law and for a job training and placement program. Many speeches were given that day. The most fa-

The 1963 March on Washington was a turning point for civil rights. (*Copyright* Washington Post; *reprinted by permission of the D.C. Public Library*)

mous one was Martin Luther King's "I Have a Dream" speech.

The March on Washington made people hopeful. But discrimination, segregation, and violence continued. Churches were bombed, civil rights workers were murdered, and the protests went on.

Early in 1964, the poll tax was finally abolished by the Twenty-Fourth Amendment to the Constitution. The following summer, the Civil Rights Act of 1964 became law. It was the strongest set of civil rights laws ever passed. The act had sections on voting, public accommodations, public facilities, education, and fair employment. It gave the Civil Rights Commission more powers. It created the Equal Employment Opportunity Commission and the Community Relations Service. It offered federal aid to schools to help them desegregate.

Passing these laws was one thing. Enforcing them was another. All over the South, black people were still being denied the right to vote. Sometimes their jobs were threatened. Many blacks failed the literacy tests, even when they were better educated than the people giving the tests. And workers who tried to help black people register were beaten and thrown into jail. Those who fought back were sometimes killed.

In 1965, Martin Luther King, Jr. was arrested during a voter registration campaign in Selma, Alabama. He said, "There are more Negroes in jail with me than there are on the voting rolls." While King was in jail, SNCC invited Malcolm X to come speak. Malcolm X was known as a militant black leader, who believed that freedom had to be won "by any means necessary." He told the crowd that whites should be thankful for King, because not all black leaders believed in nonviolence.

There were many demonstrations in Selma. One of them was by the Concerned White Citizens of Alabama. They wanted the country to know that not all whites supported segregation. They condemned the violent attacks on peaceful demonstrators. This group was very nearly attacked, too, but managed to get away before anyone was hurt.

In March, 500 people began a protest march from Selma to Montgomery. State troopers and sheriff's deputies attacked them with tear gas, billy clubs, and whips. Nearly two weeks later, King led a second Selma march. This time, President Lyndon Johnson sent Army troops, FBI agents, federal marshals, and the Alabama National Guard to protect the marchers. At the end of the five-day march, 50,000 people attended a rally at the Alabama capitol.

Segregationists especially resented other whites who took part in civil rights protests. During the first Selma attack, a white minister named James Reeb was beaten to death. Viola Liuzzo was a white homemaker from Detroit who had become a civil rights worker. After the Montgomery rally, she was shot to death by the Ku Klux Klan.

Many blacks had already lost their lives. But their deaths rarely created the same public outrage. Stokely Carmichael, a SNCC leader, said, "It seemed to me that the movement itself was playing into the hands of racism. What you want is the nation to be upset when anybody is killed . . . but it almost [seems that] for this to be recognized, a white person must be killed."

That summer, Congress passed the Voting Rights

Act of 1965. It was designed to enforce the Fifteenth Amendment. It abolished literacy tests and other practices that discriminated against blacks, poor people, and people who were not well educated or who spoke little English. With the passage of these laws, civil rights were no longer left up to local and state governments. But the battle to change the attitudes and behaviors of the people who still believed in racial segregation and discrimination was far from over.

Eli Finer / Pathfinder Press

PERSONALITY PROFILE

Malcolm X

In 1960, the two most respected black leaders in the United States held completely opposite views. Martin Luther King, Jr., believed in integration and nonviolent resistance. Malcolm X believed in racial separation. He said that black people should defend themselves against violence by fighting back. Yet many people believe that by the time of their deaths, each of them was moving closer to the other's position.

Since Martin Luther King, Jr.'s birthday became a national holiday, most people have heard something about his life. But many people know very little about Malcolm X. And not many people think about the things they had in common.

Both men's fathers were Baptist ministers who preached against racism. Both Malcolm and Martin became religious and political leaders. And both were assassinated when they were thirty-nine years old.

Malcolm Little was born on May 19, 1925 in Omaha, Nebraska. Before he was born, the Ku Klux Klan attacked his parents' home. After his birth, the family moved to Michigan. When Malcolm was very young, they were attacked by another white terrorist group called the black Legion. He remembers the white police and firemen watching the Little home burn to the ground.

In 1931, Malcolm's father was brutally murdered. Everyone believed he was killed by the Klan. A few years later, the family was broken up. Mrs. Little ended up in a mental institution. The Little children were split up and put in foster homes.

As a young man, Malcolm became a hustler, pimp, and drug dealer. When he was twenty-one, he was sent to prison for stealing. There he discovered the teachings of the Nation of Islam, also known as Black Muslims. They believed that white people were devils. Like other Black Muslims, Malcolm replaced his last name with an X. The X stood for the true African name that blacks would never know. The Black Muslims believed that God would someday give them another name.

Malcolm X became a minister himself. Soon he was the spokesperson for the Nation of Islam. When President Kennedy was assassinated, Malcolm said that it was a case of "the chickens coming home to roost"—that white hate had caused the death of a white leader. Soon he was no longer allowed to speak as a Black Muslim.

But people all over the country, black and white, respected Malcolm. He was called the only black man in America who "could stop a race riot—or start one." He decided to start his own organization; but first, he felt he had to make a journey to Mecca.

Mecca is a holy city in the Islamic religion. All orthodox Muslims try to go to Mecca at least once in their lifetimes. During his journey, Malcolm met many other Muslims who would be considered white men in the United States. Yet all of them treated him as a brother. His views began to change. He also traveled to other parts of Africa, where he was treated as an honored guest. Malcolm returned to the United States with a new name: El-Hajj Malik El-Shabazz.

In 1965, he began the Organization of Afro-American Unity (OAAU). By then, Malcolm believed that some white people sincerely wanted to end racism. But whites were not allowed to join the OAAU. He told them to find others who believed as they did and then to teach nonviolence to racist whites. He said, "Working separately, the sincere black people and sincere white people will actually be working together."

On February 21, 1965, Malcolm was shot to death while speaking at the Audubon Ballroom in New York City. Three men who were believed to be Black Muslims were convicted of Malcolm's murder.

After Malcolm's death, many people voiced opinions about why he was assassinated. Some thought it was because he had left the Nation of Islam. Others believed his assassins had been paid by Malcolm's black political rivals. Still others suspected an international plot, because Malcolm had tried to unite black people all over the world.

Since 1964, hundreds of thousands of people have read *The Autobiography of Malcolm X.*

REVIEW QUESTIONS

1. Where did the NAACP turn its attention in 1950?
2. What landmark Supreme Court decision did _Brown v. Board of Education_ reverse?
3. Why was Emmett Till murdered?
4. Why were boycotts so effective?
5. How did events in Birmingham serve as a turning point in the civil rights movement?
6. What were the white Citizens' Councils?
7. What was abolished by the Twenty-Fourth Amendment? By the Voting Rights Act?
8. How many civil rights acts were passed from 1957 to 1965?

7 | New Phases and Faces of Protest

Why did resistance to white racism become more militant in the 1960?

What militant organizations publicly addressed the issues of racially oppressed people?

What caused the urban rebellions of the 1960s?

THE CIVIL RIGHTS MOVEMENT INFLUENCES THE ENTIRE NATION

The civil rights movement concentrated on ending segregation in the South. But it influenced people of all races throughout the United States.

In the early 1960s, Indians were organizing to demand their rights. While blacks were holding sit-ins, Indians in Washington state were holding "fish-ins" on the Nisqually River. Other Indians from around the country, including members of the National Indian Youth Council, joined in. Even though an old treaty gave them fishing rights, the state courts tried to take them away. Washington whites were doing what southern whites had always done. They simply ignored federal law.

By 1964, it was clear to northern blacks that racism existed there, too. They realized that even though they had been voting for decades, they still faced segregation and discrimination in jobs, housing, and schools.

In the North, schools were segregated because neighborhoods were segregated. When black protests began, whites organized, too. They formed organizations to keep all-white neighborhoods and "neighborhood schools." They held big meetings and marches, just as the civil rights protestors did.

REBELLIONS IN WATTS AND OTHER NEIGHBORHOODS

In a speech at Howard University, President Johnson talked about the growing tensions in black neighborhoods. He said, "In far too many ways American Negroes have been another nation: deprived of freedom, crippled by hatred, the doors of opportunity closed to hope." He talked about his plans for programs that would fight poverty, unemployment, and segregation.

Days after President Johnson signed the Civil Rights Act of 1965, armed rebellion broke out in Watts, a black section of Los Angeles, California. For five days, battles were fought between Watts residents and the police. White-owned stores were looted and burned, especially those that had a reputation for discriminating against black customers. More than 13,000 National Guard troops were called in. Machine guns were set up on corners. Roadblocks were put up. The governor of California called it "a war."

Thirty-four people were killed during the Watts rebellion. More than 1,000 people were injured. Property damage was estimated at $35 million. Two hundred businesses were destroyed and over 700 damaged. A journalist compared the scene to Germany after World War II.

In the mid-1960s, rebellions occurred in other major cities, including Detroit, Newark, Chicago, and Boston. In all, 164 outbreaks of urban violence were reported. Often they began with an incident of police violence.

BLACK POWER AND ANTIWAR PROTESTS

By this time, many blacks had started to believe that the civil rights movement would not solve the problems of black people. Young people especially began to talk about *Black Power*. Stokely Carmichael, the leader of SNCC, and Floyd McKissick, the leader of CORE, first used the term during a 1966 voter registration march in Mississippi. They meant that black people should be in control of their own organizations and their own lives. They stressed black pride. Some also believed that black people should start their own independent state. They were called Black Nationalists. White people were frightened by the idea of Black Power. They thought it meant hatred and violence against whites.

Another important change occurred among the young activist organizations. Instead of concentrating exclusively on problems in the United States, they started to see themselves as part of the world. They compared the violence of war to the violence against blacks in the United States. SNCC and CORE leaders began to protest against the Vietnam War. Six SNCC members were arrested at an army induction center in Atlanta. They were sent to prison for their actions.

WAS THE U.S. GOVERNMENT WORKING FOR OR AGAINST BLACKS?

In 1967, President Johnson appointed a commission to study the rebellions and make recommendations. In its report, the Kerner Commission blamed white racism for the urban violence. It said, "Our nation is moving toward two societies, one black, one white—separate and unequal."

The Kerner Commission made a set of recommendations for change. It said, "It is time to make good the promises of American democracy to all citizens—urban and rural, black and white, Spanish-surname, American Indian, and every minority group."

Throughout the twentieth century, each time there were urban race riots, commissions were appointed to study them. Each time the commissions reached the same conclusions. And each time, their recommendations were ignored. The same thing happened with the Kerner Commission report.

After the riots, Congress passed the Civil Rights Act of 1968. It was supposed to help end violence against blacks by making the penalties stronger. But the law did not apply to policemen, soldiers, or National Guardsmen. Another section of the law did apply to anyone who crossed a state line to start or take part in a riot. It even applied to sending mail or using telephones across state lines. According to the law, a riot was the threat of violence by three or more people. In many cases, the act was used against demonstrators instead of protecting them.

The first person prosecuted under this new act was H. Rap Brown, a SNCC leader. He made a speech in

Maryland, and soon after there was a racial disturbance. Brown was blamed for it.

Even while the government seemed to be trying to help blacks, it was really working against them. From 1956 to 1971, the FBI operated a huge campaign against "Black Nationalist hate groups." It was called the Counterintelligence Program (COINTELPRO).

The goal of COINTELPRO was to destroy black leaders and break up black organizations. It used blackmail, lies, false documents, break-ins, bugs, informants, infiltrators, and even murder. At first the program's main target was Martin Luther King, Jr. and other civil rights activists. FBI agents even secretly tried to make King commit suicide. In the 1960s, organizations such as SNCC, SCLC, the Black Panthers, and the Nation of Islam were also targets.

BLACK MUSLIMS, BLACK PANTHERS, AND THE RED GUARD

The Nation of Islam was founded during the Depression. Its leader was named Elijah Muhammed, and his followers were called Black Muslims. They believed that blacks should separate from whites. They started their own businesses and encouraged other blacks to become independent. In the 1960s, when Malcolm X became the main spokesperson for the Nation of Islam, Black Muslims became well known all over the country. Muhammed Ali, who first won the heavyweight boxing championship in 1964, also brought public attention to the Nation of Islam.

The Black Panther party was started in 1966 in California. The Panthers tried to protect the black community. They said that blacks should get guns and defend themselves. Sometimes they got into gunfights with the police. The Panthers set up community schools that taught black people to be proud of their race and culture. They also ran free breakfast and lunch programs for children.

The Chinese in California also faced police brutality. A group of Chinese youth called the Red Guard modeled themselves after the Panthers. Like the Panthers, they tried to protect their community. They also started several community projects. One of them was a breakfast program for the children of Chinatown.

THE CHICANO MOVEMENT

The Mexican American movement was very much like the black movement. After the Second World War, Mexican American organizations stressed political action and civil rights. They urged their members to become loyal Americans.

In the 1960s, however, many young Mexican Americans began to call themselves *Chicanos*. They valued their Indian and Mexican heritage, instead of thinking of themselves as Spanish. They demanded control of their own institutions. They demanded the right to speak Spanish in schools and churches. And they were willing to engage in direct action to get those rights.

In 1965, Rudolfo "Corky" Gonzales organized the Crusade for Justice in Denver, Colorado. The crusade was a militant civil rights group. It worked to improve education and housing for Chicanos. It tried to stop police brutality against them.

Another well-known Chicano activist was Cesar Chavez. He headed the United Farm Workers (UFW)

Organizing Committee. In 1965, the UFW began a grape boycott to protest low wages and unsafe working conditions. The boycott gained so much support over the next three years that it became an issue in the 1968 presidential campaign.

There were many other leaders of the Chicano movement. Two in particular had a major influence. Reies Tijerina organized the Federal Alliance of Free Cities. He tried to get lands in New Mexico returned to Chicanos. José Gutierrez was the organizer of La Raza, which became a very powerful political party in Texas.

Many older Mexican Americans were very critical of the Chicano movement, just as many civil rights leaders were critical of the Black Power movement.

But Martin Luther King, Jr. refused to condemn the young militants. He said, "These are revolutionary times."

King still believed in nonviolence. But he also understood the anger and frustration that came from black ghettoes, *barrios*, Chinatowns, and reservations. He thought that it was time to go from civil rights to human rights. And so, he publicly criticized the U.S. government for waging war against Vietnam. He tried to organize poor people of all races for a poor people's march on Washington.

King's views were very unpopular. He was assassinated on April 4, 1968. Although James Earl Ray, a white man, was convicted of killing King, many believed that a powerful group of unknown people had ordered the assassination.

King was murdered four months before the march, but it went on as planned. Corky Gonzales and José Gutierrez took part in King's Poor People's Campaign. They were among the thousands who carried it on after his death.

In 1969, Chicano youth organized a huge antiwar demonstration in Los Angeles, California. Police attacked the crowd. A Chicano journalist was killed. A riot followed in which hundreds were injured and hundreds were jailed.

INDIAN PROTESTS IN THE 1970S

Some Indians who served in the Vietnam War came home to fight for Indian rights. Sid Mills was a veteran who became a leader in the Nisqually River fishing rights dispute. He said, "I owe and swear my first allegiance to Indian People in the sovereign rights of our many Tribes."

Many important Indian protests took place in the 1970s. Most of them were over broken treaty rights. In 1973, several hundred Oglala Lakota took over the town of Wounded Knee, where a group of Sioux had been massacred in 1890. They wanted the government to honor the Fort Laramie Treaty of 1868. Members of the American Indian Movement (AIM) joined them.

Just as COINTELPRO targeted black activists, it also attacked Indian activists. Within hours, hundreds of federal marshals, FBI agents, and BIA police had blockaded the town. They began to shoot at the people inside. The Pentagon later sent machine guns, grenade launchers, helicopters, and other weapons. When food supplies ran low, Indians from other states tried to deliver some food to the people at Wounded Knee. They were arrested.

The attack on Wounded Knee drew the attention of the entire world. After seventy-one days the United States agreed to negotiate. One hundred twenty people were arrested. Charges against them were later dismissed because the government had lied under oath, tampered with evidence, used illegal wiretaps, and committed several other illegal acts. The government then decided that even though the treaty was valid, it could still take Indian land.

One woman who was at Wounded Knee said, "The longest war that the U.S. government has ever waged has been against the American Indians. The war has never ceased."

PERSONALITY PROFILE

Leonard Peltier

The American Indian Movement (AIM) was started in 1968 by George Mitchell, Dennis Banks, Clyde Bellecourt, and Eddie Benton Banai. All of them are Anishinabi (Ojibwa, also known as Chippewa). By 1970 AIM was involved in almost every major Indian protest action. That was when Leonard Peltier joined the organization.

Peltier is an Anishinabi/Lakota. He was born in 1944 on the Turtle Mountain Reservation in North Dakota. In the late 1950s the government tried to get Indians to leave the reservations for the cities. As a teenager, Peltier joined his relatives in the Pacific Northwest.

In 1970, he joined AIM organizers at Fort Lawson in Seattle, Washington. Fort Lawson was an abandoned military base. It was on land that legally belonged to Indians, who demanded to have it given back. After the Fort Lawson protest, Peltier became active with AIM

Peltier's involvement with AIM made him a target of the FBI. In Milwaukee, he was beaten by two off-duty policeman, who then charged him with attempted murder. He spent five months in jail. When he got out on bond, he went into hiding. Later, he was found innocent of the charges. It turned out that the FBI was responsible for the incident.

In 1973, a group of FBI agents moved onto the Pine Ridge Reservation in South Dakota. Under FBI direction, Indian people were terrorized. In particular, AIM members and supporters were assaulted and some of them were killed. In 1975, AIM established a camp there on the property of the Jumping Bull family.

According to an AIM member, a shootout began when two FBI agents tried to "serve a warrant they didn't have on someone who wasn't there for a crime over which they had no jurisdiction." Two hundred federal troops were involved. The two agents and an AIM member were killed.

Peltier and three others were charged in the agents' deaths. The first two were found not guilty. Evidence about the FBI's action convinced the jury that they had acted in self-defense. The case against the third man was dismissed.

Peltier escaped to Canada, but he was brought back for trial. This time, the jury was not allowed to hear about FBI misconduct on the reservation. Witnesses were coerced into lying. The FBI lied about its evidence. Peltier was convicted of two murders and sentenced to two consecutive life terms in prison.

Peltier is still in prison. He has received attention from millions of people around the world who have written letters or signed petitions to try to get him a new trial. They include the archbishop of Canterbury, Archbishop Desmond Tutu, fifty-one members of Congress, and fifty-one members of the Canadian Parliament.

REVIEW QUESTIONS

1. What did Black Power mean to blacks? To whites?
2. What was the purpose of COINTELPRO?

3. What did the Kerner Commission say was the cause of urban unrest and rebellion?
4. What organization modeled itself after the Black Panthers?
5. How was the Civil Rights Act of 1968 used to deter militant protest? Who was the first person prosecuted under the act?
6. How did the Chicano movement differ from earlier Mexican American social and political movements?
7. What event called world attention to the condition of contemporary Indians?

8 Contemporary Issues

How does institutional racism affect American society?

How has the U.S. population changed in recent years?

Is racism only an American problem?

If suddenly one morning, everyone in the United States woke up with no memory of racial prejudice, would relationships between people of different races improve? Probably. Would racism be eliminated? Probably not—not unless the change in attitudes caused a change in behaviors, and the change in behaviors caused a dramatic change in customs and laws.

A 1990 Roper survey reported that U.S. citizens are less prejudiced now than they were in 1978. The survey questioned both blacks and whites about living conditions in their own neighborhoods. It asked their opinions on opportunities for blacks in housing, education, jobs, and other areas. The survey concluded that whites are now more tolerant of blacks and Hispanics, and that blacks are more satisfied with their lives.

Another survey asked college freshmen if better racial understanding was important to them. A third

of them said it was. When they were se
were asked the same question. This time, 80 percent
of them said "yes."

Some people point to these surveys as proof that
there is less racism now than there used to be. But
racism is not prejudiced feelings; it is prejudiced
behavior. Even though people may feel less prejudiced, racial discrimination is increasing.

Surveys and discussions about racism almost always mention housing, education, crime, and other
controversial social issues. That's because these issues usually affect people of color more than others.
There is a great deal of debate over whether racism is
the cause of these problems. This chapter will exam-
ine some of these issues.

DEFINING AND TAKING RESPONSIBILITY FOR RACISM

It might be helpful to begin the discussion by review-
ing the definitions of *racism* presented in the Introduction. When racial prejudice is combined with the
power to discriminate against any and all members of
that group, it's called *racism*. When a system such as
a school or court is set up to provide advantages to
one group of people at the expense of another, it's
called *institutional racism*.

Institutional racism exists because of the acts of
many individuals who either make and carry out
discriminatory practices, or allow them to continue.
Intention is not a necessary ingredient in racism.
Intended or not, it is the *effect* of a law, practice, or
behavior that determines whether it is racist.

Changing attitudes about race is important. But
racism cannot be eliminated without changing the

behaviors, practices, and laws—the institutions—that support it.

Whose responsibility is it to eliminate racism? Should it be the government's? In a 1988 *Newsweek* poll, 71 percent of the blacks who were questioned said the government was doing too little. Only 29 percent of the whites who were polled agreed. Traditionally, most blacks have believed that racism was the cause of most black problems. They have also believed that government programs should play a major role in solving these problems.

Should the people who are affected by these problems take responsibility for themselves? William J. Wilson, a black sociologist, believes that racism has created certain disadvantages. He has concluded, though, that the civil rights movement promoted racial equality and created many more opportunities. Wilson believes that economic issues, not racism, are now the real causes of black problems. He does accept the idea of government help in solving social and economic problems.

Thomas Pettigrew, a white social psychologist, has studied the effects of race and class on immigrant groups. Pettigrew has concluded that the importance of class is growing. He still believes, though, that race is the most important cause of black problems.

A small group of black intellectuals believe that race is not a factor in whether or not people can be successful. They say that social class and family stability are far more important than race. They reject the idea of government assistance for black people. This group is known as the *black neoconservatives*.

Many people who work on issues of racism think that the situation cannot be improved by concentrating on people of color as the problem. They say that racism is a white problem. They think that white people must take responsibility for making positive changes.

RACIAL VIOLENCE

Hate crimes are violent attacks against people for reasons such as racial or religious differences. In Los Angeles, California, hate crimes increased by 41 percent between 1987 and 1989. In Boston, the increase was 33 percent; in Pennsylvania, 28 percent. In New York City, the number of hate crimes doubled in just one year. Other cities all across the United States also reported big increases in hate crimes.

Anti-Semitic acts have increased. There were 1,432 reported by the Anti-Defamation League (ADL) in 1989. That was the highest number in eleven years.

Sometimes these acts are committed by white supremacist groups, many of which use weapons and warfare. These groups include the Order, Aryan Nations, Posse Comitatus, the Covenant, the Sword and the Arm of the Lord, and Church of Jesus Christ Christian. In the past decade, some of these groups have been responsible for bank robberies, murders, and other violent crimes.

In April 1990, Congress passed the Hate Crime Statistics Act. It required the Justice Department to keep track of hate crimes. It also set up a telephone hotline for people to call in information. Within two months, the hotline had taken over 1,800 calls.

The Klanwatch Project is a group that monitors the actions of the Ku Klux Klan and other hate groups. It noted a 149 percent increase in hate crimes in two

The American Nazi party targeted African-Americans and Jews in its hate campaigns. (Courtesy of The Library of Congress)

years. The project counted 289 violent acts in 1989 alone.

Police around the country are most troubled by gangs of young whites called *skinheads*. There are skinhead groups in at least 100 cities. Skinheads are know for violently attacking people of color, Jews, homosexuals, and even rival groups of skinheads. The ADL estimated that there were about 3,000 skinheads in 1990.

But many hate crimes are committed by young people who are not part of organized groups. Seventy percent of the people arrested in New York City for hate crimes are under nineteen years old. Forty percent are under sixteen.

Two of the most famous hate crimes in recent years

both happened in New York. The first was in 1986, in an all-white neighborhood in Howard Beach, Queens. Three young black men were driving through the neighborhood when their car broke down. They were attacked and chased by a group of white youths. One of the black men was run over and killed by a car as he tried to get away.

In 1989 Yusuf Hawkins, a young black man, went to look at a used car in a white neighborhood in Brooklyn called Bensonhurst. He was mobbed and beaten to death. Joseph Fama, a nineteen-year-old, was convicted of his murder. It was the first time in the history of New York state that a white person had ever been convicted of a murder charge in the death of a black person.

One reason for the increase in racial violence is economic problems. Whenever the nation is faced with hard times, racial violence increases. The people with the least economic and political power become the easiest targets. That has been true throughout the history of the United States.

In the past few years there has been an increase in hostility and violence between blacks and immigrants from other countries who live or work in black neighborhoods. Incidents have been reported in Atlanta, Milwaukee, Chicago, Los Angeles, and other cities. In January 1990, blacks organized a picket of two Korean grocery stores in Brooklyn, New York. They began after a black Haitian woman said she was attacked by the manager of one of the stores.

Later that year, three Vietnamese men were beaten by a group of blacks in Brooklyn. At first the police linked the incident to the grocery store picket. Mayor David Dinkins compared it to the lynch mobs in the

South following slavery. Eventually the police discovered that the violent incident had not begun as a racial attack.

In 1989, riots broke out in Miami, Florida. They began when a Hispanic police officer shot a black motorcyclist. There were also racial conflicts between Miami's blacks and Hispanics in 1980, 1982, and 1990.

Around the country, groups of people are organizing to ease racial tensions. In Los Angeles, an African American-Korean American group was formed. Some residents of Bensonhurst established a group to try to change their community's racist image. In 1988, over 12,000 people came to all-white Forsyth County, Georgia. They marched to protest an earlier attack by the Klan on civil rights activists who were honoring Martin Luther King, Jr. Day. The Forsyth march was then the largest civil rights demonstration since the 1960s.

THE CHANGING POPULATION

Beginning in the late 1960s blacks, Indians, Hispanics, Asians, and other people of color were referred to as *minorities*. This term was originally used because each of these groups was outnumbered in the United States by whites. Sometimes women were referred to as minorities, even though they outnumbered men. That was because the term had come to be applied to any group that faced discrimination or had no power.

Over time, people began to question the use of the term. Some rejected it because it implied that these groups were less than whites. Others noted that as the number of people of color in the United States grew, it was becoming less and less accurate to call them minorities.

In 1968, the Kerner Commission named eleven major cities where blacks would be in the majority by the 1980s. That prediction has mostly come true. In many western and southwestern cities, Hispanics already outnumber other groups. For instance, in San Antonio, Texas, Hispanics make up 51 percent of the population. Hispanics, also known as Latinos, are the fastest-growing group in the nation. A smaller but growing group is Asian. Nearly half of all immigrants to the United States are Asians. The U.S. Census Bureau predicts that by 2056, whites will be in the minority.

These changes in population are a fact of life. What remains to be seen is how society will change along with the population. Some changes are designed to help everyone take part in society. Other changes are intended to maintain racial inequality.

Society has instituted both kinds of changes with respect to language. For many people, especially recent immigrants, English is a second language. In some places, government services are now offered in several languages to assist these individuals. On the other hand, at least sixteen states have passed "English only" laws, which make English the official language for all government business. This means that such practices as printing documents in two languages are illegal. So is providing interpreters for people who don't speak English. Most of the cities and states that have passed "English only" laws have a large Hispanic population.

"English only" laws can be used as an example of how racism has been made into law. These laws are usually a sign of racial fear. Many whites are afraid that immigrants and people of color will gain political power.

RACE AND POLITICS

Just as the Kerner Commission predicted, more people of color are now holding elective office. By 1984, 3,128 elected officials were Hispanic and 5,606 were black. By 1990, there were 7,370 black elected officials. Blacks still make up only 1.5 percent of all elected officials. Nearly 70 percent of them live in the South. In 1986, Michael Espy was elected to Congress from Mississippi. It was the first time since Reconstruction that Mississippi voters had elected a black representative.

In 1990 there were more than 300 black mayors. A dozen of them govern large, urban cities. They are often used as examples of how much political power blacks have gained. One example is David Dinkins, who became mayor of New York, the country's largest city, in 1989.

But most of these mayors have more problems than power. Most came into office in the 1980s. During those years, federal support to cities declined. So did the number of jobs. At the same time, as the cities have grown old, the cost of maintaining them has risen. Many middle- and upper-income families have left the cities. That has left the burden of supporting the cities on the poor. With fewer resources, the quality of city services has decreased. Crime has increased. This pattern was also predicted by the Kerner Commission report.

On the same day Dinkins was elected, Douglas

Wilder became the first and only black elected governor. Before becoming governor of Virginia, Wilder served as a state senator and as lieutenant governor. Before he entered politics, Wilder practiced law. He said, "I was never a political activist. I was a lawyer." In the 1960s he defended civil rights activists and handled several city desegregation cases. Forty percent of Virginia's white voters supported Wilder for governor.

From 1982 to 1986, Toney Anaya was governor of New Mexico. He was the nation's first Hispanic governor. As governor, he was very outspoken about issues that concerned people of color. As chairman of Hispanic Force '84, he worked with other Hispanic leaders to reach the nation's six million voting-age Mexicans, Puerto Ricans, Cubans, and South and Central Americans. He said, "The hands that pick our lettuce, the hands that pick our cotton, are the hands that can pick the next president." Anaya had served since 1974 as New Mexico's attorney general.

In 1984 and in 1988, Reverend Jesse Jackson ran unsuccessfully for president of the United States. It was the first time that a person of color had been a serious presidential candidate. His support came from a group called the Rainbow Coalition. It was made up mostly of people of color, liberal white political activists, and poor or working-class whites. In 1990, Jackson began representing the District of Columbia as a nonvoting member of the United States Senate.

Whites with a history of racist behavior are also being elected to public office. The most well-known one is David Duke. In 1988 he was elected to the Louisiana House of Representatives. Duke was a former grand wizard of the Ku Klux Klan. After his election, there was evidence that Duke continued to maintain strong ties with white supremacist organizations, although he publicly denied it. In 1990 Duke ran for U.S. Senate. He received 44 percent of the vote. His campaign for "affirmative action for whites" and "upholding Western European, Christian values" appealed to many white voters.

Tom Metzger, a skinhead leader and organizer, ran for Congress in 1980. He won the California Democratic primary race but lost in the general election. In 1982 he ran for the U.S. Senate. He got 75,000 votes.

Often black or Hispanic voters have less impact as a group because their neighborhoods are *gerrymandered*. This means that they are deliberately divided among several voting districts. This practice began in Mississippi in 1876, during Reconstruction. In order to prevent the reelection of John R. Lynch, a black man, Mississippi created a mostly white congressional district that was 500 miles long and forty miles wide. The Supreme Court outlawed racial gerrymandering in 1960 in the case of *Gomillion v. Lightfoot*.

Gerrymandering is also a violation of the Voting Rights Act. The law was tested in 1986 in *Thornburg v. Gingles*. The Supreme Court ruled that the way black communities in North Carolina were divided was illegal. The following year, blacks in Springfield, Illinois won a class action suit against the city. Because of segregation and the city's at-large election process, no black had been elected to the city council since 1911. The suit outlawed at-large elections in Springfield.

In 1990, a federal judge ordered that the five districts of Los Angeles County, California be reshaped.

About 35 percent of the people in the county are Hispanic. Yet no Hispanic candidate had been elected to the county's Board of Supervisors since 1875. In response to the court order, the board came up with a plan that would make Hispanics the majority in one of the districts.

ECONOMICS

Today the black middle class is larger than it has ever been. But overall, black people are poorer now than in the 1950s. Thirty-three percent of blacks in the United States are poor. Twenty-eight percent of Latinos are poor. Among Asians, the poverty rate is 13 percent, ranging from 7 percent for Japanese to 35 percent for Vietnamese. For Indians, it is more than double the national average. For whites, it is less than 12 percent. Children make up most of the poor. Half of all black children live in poverty.

People of color are beginning to use their spending power to force some changes. In the 1960s, local boycotts helped desegregate buses, lunch counters, and other public facilities. But in 1969, merchants in Port Gibson, Mississippi successfully sued the NAACP for $3.5 million dollars because of a boycott there. For a while, there were few boycotts. But in 1982, the Supreme Court overturned the Port Gibson decision. The Court said that citizens have a right to use boycotts as a protest weapon. In the 1980s and 1990s, boycotts have gotten bigger. Today, the main issue is often economic development in communities of color.

In Miami, several racial incidents led to a tourism boycott in the summer of 1990. Black lawyers in

Miami decided against hosting the National Bar Association conference there. They urged other groups to also boycott Miami's convention facilities. In the first six months of the boycott, Miami lost between $4.5 million and $13.5 million in tourist dollars. Discrimination against blacks in employment and other areas has always been an issue in Miami. One of the conditions for ending the boycott is an increase in employment and business opportunities in tourism for blacks. One of the boycott leaders said, "We finally realized that the helping hand we were looking for is at the other end of our own arm."

In 1990, Arizona voted against making Martin Luther King, Jr.'s birthday a state holiday. As a result, the National Football League threatened to take the 1993 Superbowl somewhere else instead of coming to Arizona. Many college teams decided to boycott sports events there, too.

In 1990, black people protested against the Professional Golf Association (PGA) for holding a major tournament at the Shoal Creek Country Club in Alabama. Shoal Creek's membership policies specifically excluded black people (the PGA itself had a "Caucasians only" policy until 1961). Several large corporations such as IBM decided not to advertise during the tournament. They were afraid that they would become the targets of bad publicity or economic boycotts. After these sponsors withdrew, the club decided to change its policy. Just before the tournament began, it offered membership to an elderly black man who hadn't played golf in twenty years.

The same month, the PGA announced its own new policy against holding events at clubs that discriminate by race, religion, or sex. At least three clubs pulled out of the PGA rather than change their rules. Many people were still critical of the PGA, because even after the new ruling, some events were still scheduled at segregated clubs. They also pointed out that the PGA knew all along about these clubs' discriminatory policies but didn't act until big businesses began to pull out.

Should big businesses take more responsibility? Many large corporations feel that they must. There are fewer people entering the work force. More of them are people of color. Companies are having a hard time finding enough good employees because the public education system has done such a poor job. Some companies have started their own programs to teach employees reading, writing, and other basic skills. In 1990, Ford Motor Company spent over $200 million dollars on education and training programs.

Hundreds of companies have started programs that recruit, train, and promote women and people of color. Called "Managing Diversity," these programs try to meet the needs of many different kinds of employees. They also try to change unfair attitudes and practices in the workplace. One unfair practice is called the *glass ceiling:* women and people of color are recruited into management positions but are rarely promoted into the highest positions.

College-educated Asians face a special problem. It is usually easy for them to find well-paying jobs at the entry level, especially in technical fields. But it is very difficult for them to get into management, administration, or executive positions. The head of a Chinese American organization said, "In the past, we had the coolie who slaved. Today we have the high-tech coolie." Diversity programs try to help companies make the best use of all their employees' skills.

Besides getting good employees, diversity progams have helped some companies increase their business. For instance, Avon, the cosmetics company, saw a tremendous increase in their sales when black and Hispanic sales managers took charge of inner-city markets.

SEGREGATION IN HOUSING AND EDUCATION

Housing is more segregated today than in 1960. Blacks are still not welcome in many areas. According to the Klanwatch Project, the most common hate crimes are against families of color who move into white neighborhoods. They made up 45 percent of the cases documented by Klanwatch in 1989. Incidents included threats, vandalism, arson, and assault.

A 1988 study by the University of Chicago said that residential integration is possible, even likely, for all racial and ethnic groups *except* blacks. No matter how well educated they are, how much money they make, or what kinds of jobs they have, blacks are more segregated than any other race.

This means that most middle-class blacks pay more to live in neighborhoods with higher crime rates, worse schools, and more dilapidated surroundings than middle-class whites. The study also found that dark-skinned Latinos are more segregated than white Latinos.

One cause of housing segregation is *redlining*. That means that banks and other lenders won't finance home mortgages in certain areas. Redlining is unfair and illegal. Court cases and investigations by community groups have found redlining in Boston, Chicago, Dallas, Detroit, Philadelphia, Washington, D.C., and Columbus, Ohio. The Community Reinvestment Act, passed in 1977, prohibits redlining. It requires banks to lend to groups of low- and middle-income people who've been excluded from the housing market, to minority-owned businesses, and to small businesses. Another widespread practice is *housing covenants,* where real estate brokers agree not to sell houses in certain areas to blacks. Sometimes redlining results from these agreements.

In 1986, an important Supreme Court case linked housing discrimination and school segregation. A group of black parents in Kansas City, Missouri proved that both public and private institutions were creating and maintaining segregated neighborhoods. Real estate agents sold homes to blacks only in certain areas. State banking institutions refused housing loans to blacks. State agencies discriminated in selecting public housing sites. As a result, Kansas City schools were segregated. The Court ordered the state to spend $300 million on programs that would create better educational opportunities for blacks.

In 1989, the National School Board Association warned that public schools are becoming more and more segregated for Hispanics and blacks. Some areas are as segregated as they were before 1970, when large-scale busing began. The association reported that most Asian students do not attend segregated schools.

Today, two-thirds of all black students attend predominantly black schools. That is about the same rate as in 1965. Seventy percent of Latino students attend predominantly Latino schools. In major cities, nearly 60 percent of all children in public schools are black or Latino.

EDUCATION

For many years, public school systems were expected to spend the same amount of money on all schools. In the past few years, however, some courts have said that it is legal for wealthier districts to get more money. Differences in spending and patterns of segregation mean that in many places, schools are once again separate and unequal.

Test scores and other measures say the schools are not doing a good job of educating most children of color. Asians, Hispanics, Indians, and blacks get lower scores on the Scholastic Aptitude Test than whites. The average score for blacks is 200 points lower than the average score for whites. The longer blacks and Latinos stay in school, the farther they fall behind.

A 1989 report by the Joint Center for Political Studies said that these children perform poorly because schools expect less from them. The report also mentions other problems, such as the high number of black children who are put into special education programs. Inner-city schools often have inadequate resources, such as no science labs and outdated textbooks. And few people of color take part in decisions about how schools and classes are run.

In 1989, a group of Hispanics in California filed suit with the Civil Rights Division of the U.S. Education Department. Schools in the San Joaquin Valley have large Hispanic populations. In some schools, Hispanics are in the majority by as much as 90 percent. However, there are very few Hispanic teachers. Most of the schools have very few Hispanic counselors or administrators. Many have none.

Several projects have shown that community involvement and high expectations can change student performance. In 1968, the Yale Child Study Center adopted two schools in New Haven, Connecticut. Ninety percent of the students were children of color from poor backgrounds. The schools had the worst attendance records, behavior problems, and achievement levels in the city. As part of the project, parents, teachers, and staff formed teams that governed the schools. By 1984, the two schools had the second and third highest achievement levels in the city. They also had the best attendance records.

In the 1960s a preschool program called Head Start was begun for poor children. Head Start has been very effective in giving children the academic and social skills they need to succeed in school. The number of poor children is increasing, but during the mid-1980s, the amount of money going into Head Start did not increase. In 1990, a $500 million increase was proposed for Head Start, but was later rejected. Even if it had passed, it would have been enough for only 27 percent of the children who are eligible.

Other programs that began in the 1960s, such as Upward Bound and A Better Chance, Inc. (ABC), have also been drastically cut. Upward Bound helps low-income high school students prepare for college. ABC is an extremely successful program that helps promising inner-city students get into academically challenging high schools, most of them prestigious boarding schools. Both Upward Bound and ABC mostly serve students of color.

Overall, the number of high school dropouts in the United States has decreased. For students of color, it is increasing. In Boston, Chicago, Detroit, and Los Angeles, dropout rates are between 44 percent and 85 percent for blacks, Hispanics, and Indians. Most dropouts are poor. Many of them, especially boys, drop out so that they can get a job. However, most of the jobs available to dropouts pay very little. Many dropouts end up involved in street crime.

CRIME AND LAW ENFORCEMENT

A 1990 report by the Sentencing Project said that nearly 25 percent of all young black men end up in the criminal justice system. For Hispanic men, the figure is about 10 percent. For white men, it is about 6 percent.

The United States puts more people in prison than any other country in the world. For every 100,000 people in the United States, 426 were in jail in 1990. In western Europe, the rate was between 35 and 120.

White people in the United States go to prison at about the same rate as western Europeans. But imprisonment rates for blacks in the United States are the highest in the world—four times the rate of South Africa! Black men make up almost half of the U.S. prison population. Black men in the United States are more likely to go to prison than to college.

Statistics from all over the nation say that there is racial discrimination in sentencing. For instance, in Georgia, 11 percent of all people who are charged with killing whites receive the death penalty. Only 1 percent of the people charged with killing blacks receive the death penalty. When the person charged with the killing is black and the victim is white, prosecutors ask for the death penalty in 70 percent of these cases. About half of the prisoners on death row are people of color.

Several well-known criminologists such as William Nagel have found that large numbers of people go to jail because of their race. Their studies show that the number of blacks in prison depends on how many live in an area, not on how much crime there is. The same is true for other people of color. These criminologists say that the criminal justice system is used to control the population during times of economic or political trouble.

The Kerner Commission report recommended that more money be spent on education, training, and employment for inner-city youth. Otherwise, it warned, street crime would cost much, much more. Instead, these programs were cut. At the same time, there were huge increases in the Justice Department budget. According to Charles Ogletree, a professor of law at Harvard University, the United States spends $7 billion a year to imprison black males, but less than 10 percent of that amount to educate black males.

Chicago, Los Angeles, Indianpolis, and Washington, D.C. are trying to find alternatives to prison. They evaluate some offenders to decide what kind of counseling, education, or training might help them. Then they come up with community service programs. The court then decides whether these offenders should go to jail or go into these programs. The decision is based on what seems best for the community.

Another criminal justice issue for people of color is how they are treated by the police. Nearly every urban riot from the 1960s to the 1980s began when the police killed someone. Until 1982, the Law Enforcement Assistance Administration was responsible for nationwide programs to investigate police abuse. Then it was dismantled by the Reagan administration. Since then, citizens groups in New York, Chicago, Philadelphia, and many other cities have tried other approaches. They monitor police activities. They try to pass laws against police misconduct. They take police officers and police departments to court in abuse cases.

In March of 1991, a case of police brutality in California gained national attention. Following a car chase, Los Angeles police officers stopped a young black man named Rodney King for speeding. King was shot with a stun gun, clubbed, stomped, and kicked at least 50 times by four officers while eight others watched. King's skull was broken in nine places. A man who lived nearby videotaped the scene from his balcony. Soon after, the tape was shown on national television.

Nearly two weeks later, the four officers who beat King were indicted on criminal charges. King also filed a $56 million civil suit against the Los Angeles Police Department. According to Police Chief Donald Gates, the city paid more than $10 million in damages to victims of police misconduct in 1990. That same year, there were more than 600 citizens' complaints against Los Angeles police. A former president of the

Los Angeles Civil Service Commission estimated that five times as many complaints go unreported.

In many cities, hiring and promotion practices have been challenged. As a result, more people of color have become police officers. A lawsuit in Detroit proved that having more black police benefited everyone. Relationships between blacks and whites improved. Fewer officers were killed or injured, and more homicide cases were solved.

AFFIRMATIVE ACTION

Racial violence and discrimination have increased as civil rights laws and policies have been weakened. In 1964 and 1965, laws were passed against discrimination in jobs and education. That was the beginning of _affirmative action_. But Ronald Reagan, who became president in 1980, did not believe in affirmative action, civil rights legislation, or other government measures that oppose discrimination. He never supported even one civil rights issue and often spoke out against measures that others attempted.

During his eight-year administration, Reagan appointed 380 federal judges. He also nominated three justices to the Supreme Court who shared his political views. Until the mid-1980s the Supreme Court took a strong stand in support of affirmative action laws. In recent years, however, the Court has made several decisions that weaken the laws.

Affirmative action means that employers do more than just agree not to discriminate. They must also try to correct past discrimination by giving preference to people of color, women, and the disabled. Affirmative action also applies to education and to government contracts.

When a company has to reduce its size, the people who have worked there the longest are usually allowed to keep their jobs. Since many companies only recently began hiring women and people of color, they have the least amount of seniority and are usually the first to be let go. This practice is sometimes referred to as "last hired, first fired." Some affirmative actions plans are designed to address this problem.

In 1986, the Supreme Court rejected such a plan by a Michigan public school system. The system hired its first black teacher in 1953. Sixteen years later, less than 4 percent of the teachers were black. In order to keep as many black teachers as possible, the school board came up with a plan that protected them during layoffs. In *Wygant v. Jackson Board of Education*, the Court said that affirmative action plans cannot substitute for seniority.

Some people think that affirmative action policies are unfair. They believe that it gives some groups an unfair advantage. They say that affirmative action is *reverse discrimination*. By that they mean that it discriminates against whites by hiring less qualified people of color. They think that no one should be given preference, and that everyone should have an equal chance. Many people believe that affirmative action really doesn't work anyway.

People who support affirmative action say that without it, the most qualified people often don't get an equal chance. Whites with high school diplomas still earn more than blacks with college degrees. Men still earn more than twice as much as women. Companies with affirmative action plans usually hire and promote two or three times as many women and people of color as companies without them. Companies with such plans say that all their employees have benefited from affirmative action. It has helped them improve their hiring, promotion, and performance review processes for everyone.

In 1989, the Supreme Court decided several cases that weakened employment discrimination laws. In *Price v. Waterhouse*, the Court ruled that hiring decisions based partly on prejudice are legal if the employer can prove that the decisions would have been the same even without the element of prejudice. Another decision was that discrimination is illegal in hiring but is legal once a person is hired. *Wards Cove v. Atonio* made individuals responsible for proving that they had been discriminated against; in the past, companies had to prove that they were not discriminating. Still other decisions made it more difficult for local governments to establish affirmative action plans in hiring and awarding contracts.

Just as racial discrimination hurts everyone, the solutions often benefit everyone. In 1987, a professor sued St. Francis College because he was denied tenure. He said that he had been discriminated against because he had been born in Iraq. The college claimed that the law against racial discrimination did not apply to him because he was white.

When the case went to the Supreme Court, the Court noted that even though Arabs and Jews are considered white now, they were not in the 1800s when the law was written. The Court ruled that the law was intended to protect all people who are discriminated against because of their racial, ethnic, or religious backgrounds, including whites.

In education, affirmative action is used to increase the number of people of color in colleges and graduate schools. The same arguments against affirmative action in hiring are also applied to college admissions.

In fact, the idea of reverse discrimination came from a school admissions case. In 1971, Michael DeFunis applied to the University of Washington Law School but was not accepted. Thirty-six students of color, who had lower grades and lower tests scores, were admitted. DeFunis, who was Jewish, claimed that he was the victim of reverse discrimination. As it turned out, thirty-eight white students with lower scores than DeFunis had also been admitted. The law school argued that other things besides grades and test scores were considered in their decisions.

DeFunis won his case in the state courts. He was admitted to the law school. Before his graduation, however, his case was overturned by the state's Supreme Court. He then appealed to the U.S. Supreme Court. The Court did not actually reach a decision about whether the law school was practicing reverse discrimination. It said that the DeFunis appeal was moot, since he was already attending the law school.

The Supreme Court did rule against reverse discrimination in 1978 in the Bakke case. Allan Bakke was a white man who sued for admission to the University of California at Davis Medical School. He argued that he had been discriminated against because his academic record was better than some minorities who had been admitted under affirmative action plans. Out of 100 available spaces, the school had reserved sixteen for minorities. The Court said that affirmative action was legal, but that _quotas_ (a certain number of spaces set aside for a particular group) were not. Bakke won his case and was admitted.

One of the biggest criticisms of affirmative action is that colleges lower their admissions standards in order to accept students of color. Some people claim that these students take places away from "more qualified" white students.

Instead, several prestigious schools report just the opposite. They say that affirmative action policies have helped them recruit the top students of color. In 1985, 20 percent of the freshman class at Harvard were students of color. They were chosen from the top third of all applicants. By 1989, 32.3 percent of Harvard's entering freshmen were students of color. Seven percent were Hispanic, 9.6 percent were black, and 15.3 percent were Asian.

Over the past few years, there has been a rising tide of anti-Asian feeling in the United States. Some of the reasons are increases in the number of Asian immigrants, Japanese economic development, and the superior academic performance of many Asian students. In some schools, a large percentage of the students of color are Asian. Asian students are sometimes viewed as the new "yellow peril" by whites who fear that they take places away from white students. In 1989, the Justice Department began investigating several schools, including Harvard and UCLA. Before the investigation, there had been charges that these schools were setting limits on the number of Asian students they admitted. The Justice

Department found evidence to support these charges.

Asian students have a reputation as hard workers. Education is valued in their cultures. Asian immigrant students often do well in math and science, because their schools and families stress these subjects. They are seen as "whiz kids," but not all of them are. Many immigrant students have trouble reading and writing in English. Half of the Filipino students at UCLA drop out before graduation. Educators worry that the educational and counseling needs of these students aren't being met.

For several years, incidents of racism on college campuses have been increasing. They are directed at all students of color, including Asians. In 1988, the National Institute Against Prejudice and Violence listed 163 incidents of racial violence over the previous two years. In 1989, 250 colleges reported incidents. The institute believes that many others were either overlooked or not reported.

According to the National Association of Student Personnel Administrators, many white students believe it is okay to feel and act in racially prejudiced ways. Much of whites' hostility toward students of color stems from resentment. They think that government policies have favored people of color. Actually, higher education programs established during the civil rights years have helped more low-income whites than blacks, Latinos, and Indians. The same is true of other kinds of social programs. For example, the Job Training Partnership Act (JTPA), passed in 1982, creates education and training programs for poor people. In the mid-1980s, at least 55 percent of the people enrolled in JTPA programs were white.

Scholarships and other kinds of financial aid have been an important part of the affirmative action policies of most colleges and universities. Once the schools have recruited a diverse student body, financial aid is offered to students who otherwise couldn't afford to attend. In 1990, a new interpretation of the 1964 Civil Rights Act put these policies in jeopardy. It came from the assistant secretary for civil rights in the Department of Education. He announced that it was illegal for colleges and universities that receive federal funds to award scholarships based on race.

Very few schools actually do give scholarships based solely on race. But many people worried about how this decision would affect college recruitment. Schools that had been committed to recruiting more students could face legal challenges. And schools that were not committed could use the decision as an excuse not to do more. This decision was unpopular with almost everyone, even President George Bush.

When President Bush took office in 1988, he promised that he would have "a positive civil rights agenda." Even though Bush has been friendlier to civil rights leaders, his policies have not been much different from Reagan's. His administration has also opposed affirmative action. After Congress passed the 1990 Civil Rights Act, Bush vetoed it.

REPARATIONS

Reparations are payments made to a group of people, usually by the government, for some past injustice. Japanese Americans, African Americans, and Native Americans are among the groups who have tried for decades to get reparations.

In 1988, the efforts of Japanese Americans were at last successful. That year Congress passed the Civil Liberties Act. The act authorized the government to pay $20,000 to every living person who was imprisoned in Japanese internment camps during the Second World War. In 1990, Congress approved $1.25 billion to finance it.

After World War II, the government offered an apology (but very little else) to the Japanese Americans who had been interned. No official apology has ever been offered for American slavery. In 1990, Congressman John Conyers, Jr. proposed a bill that would admit to the "injustice, cruelty, brutality and inhumanity of slavery in the United States." The bill would also provide money to study the effect of slavery on the economics, politics, and lives of African Americans.

The idea of reparations for African Americans has been around since the practice of slavery was ended. Following the Civil War, black freedmen believed that every former male slave would receive forty acres of land, $50, and a mule. Since then, the words *forty acres and a mule* have been a symbol of economic injustice to black people. In June of 1990, the Conference on Black Reparations was held in Washington, D.C. People who came to the conference discussed several ideas for using land and money to develop opportunities for blacks.

Giving reparations to Indian people is more controversial now than in the 1800s. Treaties between the United States and Indian nations were supposed to guarantee certain rights forever. When Indians were forced to give up their lands, they were usually given smaller areas of land that whites considered worthless. Sometimes the treaties also gave them hunting and fishing rights. But for more than 100 years, those treaties have continued to be violated. When natural resources such as gold, oil, or uranium are discovered on Indian land, the government sometimes forces the sale of the land.

Many whites are also resentful of the privileges they think Indians enjoy. They believe that Indians should have no special rights but should be treated like everyone else. President Reagan was sharply criticized in 1988 when he voiced a similar opinion during a trip to the Soviet Union. Reagan told a group of students that the United States might have "made a mistake" in allowing Indian people to maintain their own cultures. He said, "Maybe we should not have humored them in that, wanting to stay in that kind of primitive lifestyle. Maybe we should have said: 'No, come join us. Be citizens along with the rest of us.' " He also claimed that Indians became rich because of the oil on some reservations. In fact nearly half of all Indians live below the official poverty level. On some reservations, 70 percent of the people cannot find jobs.

In 1988, the Senate Select Committee on Indian Affairs spent a year investigating abuses in federal Indian programs. The committee discovered corruption, fraud, and mismanagement in the Bureau of Indian Affairs (BIA), which oversees these programs. Early in 1989, several Indian leaders testified before Congress about these problems.

Later in 1989, an audit conducted by the GAO showed that the government had mismanaged an Indian trust fund. The BIA fund managed over $1.7 billion for 200 Indian nations and nearly one million individual people. Seventeen million dollars could not be accounted for because of sloppy bookkeeping. The audit report said that the money could have been stolen. Another $19.5 million was lost because of bad investments and poor management. The audit furnished an example of the kind of negligence and exploitation of Indian people that the Senate was investigating.

In November 1989, the Senate committee issued its report. It said that Indian nations should be given more control over their land and money. In the summer of 1990, the Department of the Interior started a project to try out this idea. Six nations were given more control over how to budget and spend their share of federal funds for BIA programs.

More and more Indian nations are turning to lawmakers and to state and federal courts. In some cases, they are trying to have treaty provisions enforced. In others, they are questioning whether the treaties are actually legal. And in still others, they are claiming their rights when no treaties exist.

In 1988, three North Dakota nations tried to get a new settlement for their land. In the 1940s, their tribal lands were used to build a 200-mile-long reservoir behind Garrison Dam. The Arikara, Hidatsa, and Mandan were forced to move onto higher, less productive land. The reservoir divided their reservation into isolated sections. It also changed the people's way of life. Unemployment and alcoholism became major problems.

In 1950, the three nations were given a $12.6 million settlement. In 1986, a panel appointed by the secretary of the interior said that the Indians were still owed between $178 million and $412 million for their land. The tribes asked Congress for $178.4 million. They wanted a bill that would give them $3.6 million a year for fifty years, plus interest. They wanted to use the money for work projects, alcohol treatment, and other programs. The BIA opposed the idea. The tribes were told that they had already received enough compensation.

For nine years, the Abenaki of Vermont deliberately tried to get arrested and prosecuted for fishing and hunting without licenses. They claimed that they were the original inhabitants of Vermont, but the federal government refused to recognize them as a tribe. They wanted their cases to go to court so that they would have a legal ruling. In 1988, the state finally agreed to prosecute. In 1989 a state judge ruled that the Abenaki did not need licenses. He said that they were on the land before Vermont ever became a state, and that they had never given up their rights.

In 1990 Seneca Indians in Salamanca, New York, began renegotiating the town's lease. Salamanca is the only town in the United States built on land leased from an Indian nation. In the 1800s, it was illegally established on Seneca land. The original ninety-nine-year lease expired in February 1991.

Since 1892, the Seneca had received $17,000 a year. Some residents paid as little as $1 a year for the property they leased. But under the terms of the new lease, the Seneca demanded $800,000 a year, plus $60 million to make up for the low prices of the last century.

In 1989, there was an armed stand-off between New York state police and Mohawk on the St. Regis Reservation. The reservation is partly in New York and partly in Canada. The dispute began over whether gambling was legal on the New York side. Soon the question was whether federal law, modern tribal law, or traditional law should apply on the reservation. There was also disagreement over who had the right to enforce it.

In the summer of 1990, Canadian Mohawk were attacked by police in Oka, Quebec. The Mohawk had put up armed barricades to block expansion of a golf course. They claimed that the land was theirs. Before they took up arms, the Mohawk tried in court to block the golf course, but they lost.

In another part of Quebec, Cree Indians went to court to stop a huge hydroelectric dam project. Once completed, the project will take away land in the James Bay region which the Cree claim. The Cree lost their case. But they said that they will take up arms to prevent construction.

The Mohawk and the Cree are part of a movement by Canadian Indians and Inuit (Eskimos) to reclaim their ancestral lands. Some Indian leaders have compared the movement to the black urban riots of the 1960s.

Some of the men involved in the Oka barricade were Mohawk from the U.S. side of the reservation. Over the past decade, several Indian leaders have urged native people all over South, Central, and North America to support each other's struggles.

RACISM ABROAD

When people talk about racism in other countries, *apartheid* is almost always mentioned. *Apartheid* is an Afrikaans word. Afrikaans is one of the two official languages in the Republic of South Africa (English is the other). It is pronounced "a-part-hate."

The English translation of *apartheid* is "apartness." But apartheid is much more than that. It is a system that places control of South Africa's land and labor in the hands of its white citizens, who make up about 13 percent of the population. It is the official policy of the South African government.

South Africa is certainly not the only country that practices racism. But it is the only one that bases its entire political system on race. South African law requires all its citizens to discriminate by race. The United Nations called apartheid "a crime against humanity."

South Africa's apartheid laws could be compared to the Black Codes in the South during Reconstruction. Hundreds and hundreds of laws govern how blacks live and work "from the cradle to the grave." An important part of "Apartheid's Grand Plan" is the system of reservations for blacks, called *bantustans* or *homelands*. The bantustan system was modeled after the Indian reservation system in the United States.

For most of the 1970s and 1980s, South Africa had more trade with the United States than with any other country in the world. Many people in the United States complained to U.S. companies. They wanted them to stop doing business with South Africa. They convinced hundreds of local and state governments to get rid of stocks in companies that continued to trade with South Africa. This process is called *divestment*.

In 1986, the U.S. Congress approved economic sanctions against South Africa. President Reagan vetoed the bill, but there was still enough support to pass it over his objections. The law calls for South Africa to meet several conditions that prove it is trying to abolish apartheid. Then the sanctions will be lifted. One of those conditions was that Nelson Mandela be freed.

On February 11, 1990, the South African government released Mandela from prison. He had been there since 1961. During those years, Mandela had become one of the most famous men in the world. He was one of many South Africans who fought against apartheid. People all over the world demanded his freedom and an end to apartheid.

Even before Mandela's release, some apartheid laws had begun to change. The law against marrying someone from another race was dropped. There were fewer restrictions on where black people could live. And the pass system, which required all black adults to carry passbooks, was changed.

Many people saw these reforms as a sign of progress in South Africa. Others believed that they would mean nothing unless white South Africans agreed to share political power with blacks. Mandela's release was a sign that power-sharing might happen.

While things seemed to be getting better in South Africa, antiapartheid activists were less hopeful about the United States. They noticed that some political leaders condemned apartheid but continued to support unfair policies in the United States. For many people, the antiapartheid movement's slogan changed from "Abolish Apartheid" to "Fight Racism at Home and Abroad."

ELIMINATING RACISM

Segregation, housing, education, poverty, and urban decay are all issues that the Kerner Commission talked about. So are unemployment, crime, police brutality, and criminal justice. The Kerner Commission report concluded that all these issues are symptoms of a deeper problem. The problem, according to the Kerner Commission, is white racism. It also said that unless the United States committed itself to solving these issues, they would get bigger and more costly for society as a whole. Even if everyone agreed on the problem, though, the solutions still would not be simple.

None of these issues are new. In fact, most of them have been problems for people of color since before the United States became a nation. One major difference is that many of these problems began as the result of laws that discriminated specifically on the basis of race. Now discrimination persists despite the abolition of race-specific laws. And now these problems are so big that solutions sometimes seem impossible.

Many people question the Kerner Commission's conclusions. They wonder why they should be responsible for systems they didn't create. How, they ask, can people who weren't even alive when these problems began be held accountable for the things their ancestors did?

It may help to compare racism to pollution. Much of our land, water, and air has been poisoned for decades. Even though pollution began long before any of us were born, we all suffer the consequences now. And unless everyone—the government, business, and individuals—begins to take responsibility for stopping pollution and cleaning up the mess that has already been made, future generations will continue to suffer.

REVIEW QUESTIONS

1. Do you think race relations are better than they were in 1960? Why or why not?
2. Is there institutional racism today? What are some examples?
3. Should the government be responsible for solving the problems of institutional racism?
4. Do you believe affirmative action is helpful to everyone? Does it always result in reverse discrimination?
5. What were some of the problems the Kerner Commission report talked about? What did it say was the cause of those problems?

9 Future Outlook

Is overt, individual racism still alive?
Is racism here to stay?
Whose business is it to fight racism?

Changing attitudes about racism is the first step to ending racism. But it is only the first step. What's really important is changing behavior. Remember, a person doesn't have to intend to be racist for racism to happen. It is the outcome of a kind of behavior, practice, or law that determines whether it is racist.

Thinking about making changes can be overwhelming. One student said, "Racism is like air. It is everywhere, but it is often invisible." It may be hard for you to imagine how you can make a difference.

But you can.

You can start by looking for the little things around you that can be changed. One group of students wrote to a company that makes crayons. They asked the company to find a new name for a crayon called "flesh-colored." The students pointed out that the crayon was only flesh-colored if you're white.

Another group of students wrote to a game manufacturer. One of the games they really liked used pictures of thirty different characters. The students were concerned, though, that none of the characters were people of color. They asked the company to make some changes in its game.

When companies get letters like these, they answer them. Usually they say, "Thanks for writing, and we'll look into it." But if enough people write enough letters, they really do pay attention. And if enough people say they will boycott that company's products, the company has to think about making some changes.

Another way to change things is to get other people involved in thinking about racism. It helps to work with other people who share your concerns.

For example, a group of high school students in Ann Arbor, Michigan were worried about several incidents of racism that happened in their schools. They decided to do something about it. Their idea was to design a survey.

The students believed that just trying to change attitudes wasn't enough. They thought that it was important to find out the causes of racial problems in the Ann Arbor schools. They also wanted to find out how much racial tension there was. And they wanted to help other students start thinking about these issues. They called themselves the Anti-Racism Survey Committee.

Nearly all the high school students in Ann Arbor took part in the racism survey. The committee analyzed the results. One thing they learned was that most students believed that "separation of different groups was not bad—and, in fact, was natural." What they considered bad was segregation. They saw that people are excluded from certain groups out of fear or prejudice. They blamed social segregation on institutional racism. They mentioned segregation in housing and discrimination in class placements.

Based on the survey results, the committee made some recommendations to the school board. They requested follow-up activities, such as workshops, discussions, and assemblies in all the schools. They asked that academic tracking and other discriminatory policies be ended. (Tracking means that the school makes judgments about a student's academic ability, and from then on, that student takes courses only within a certain track. Two examples of tracks are vocational and college preparatory.) They wanted required courses on racial oppression in the United States. And they suggested that a task force be established with two responsibilities: to look at the high school curriculum from a multicultural perspective, and to make up guidelines for handling racial problems in the schools.

The school district was not ready to take up the committee's suggestions. Some of the students were discouraged. But there were some successes. One school held discussions in every class about the survey results. Two other schools had class discussions and workshops. The next year, the school board agreed to have each school plan a multicultural program.

Later, the students started another program called SEED (Students Educating Each Other About Discrimination). In the SEED program, high school students work with sixth graders. The plan is that when those sixth graders reach high school, they will join the program and continue the work.

The Anti-Racism Survey Committee believed that "schools are not set up to allow students to organize anything." Yet their hard work created programs that will continue even after they have left the schools.

Their work points out a third way to work against racism—by gaining knowledge. The more you know about a problem, the better you can understand it. And the better you understand it, the easier it is to solve it.

At the turn of the century, people called the United States "the melting pot." They thought that in the United States, everyone would lose their racial and cultural identities and become Americans. Many people believed in this idea. It was never really true, though, especially for people of color. Eleanor Roosevelt said that the nation was more like a pressure cooker than a melting pot.

Some people are still convinced that the United States should be a melting pot. Usually what they mean is that everyone should embrace Anglo-Saxon culture. They think that talking about differences will divide people, although they may be willing to admit that other races and cultures have made contributions.

But more and more people are beginning to talk about an American "stew." What they mean is that each group keeps its own identity. The "broth" is what all these groups have in common: the things that make a national identity. Each group contributes its own unique cultural "flavor" to the "broth." That's what *multiculturalism* is. A truly multicultural society recognizes that people have different beliefs, customs, and experiences. It also recognizes the importance of each of these groups.

Even some people who believe in multiculturalism don't quite understand what it means. They talk about being "tolerant" of other races and cultures. Or they think that people should be "colorblind," which means that they shouldn't see racial differences, because beneath the skin, everyone is the same.

Multiculturalism doesn't mean that everyone is the same. And it certainly doesn't mean ignoring racism, discrimination, and other social problems that result from differences among people. It means understanding how different groups have come together, frequently in conflict, to create our history and determine our future.

The United States is a nation of many *different* people. And in the history of the United States, people have always been discriminated against for being different. That may be why European immigrants wanted very much to believe in the melting pot. In the past many immigrants changed their names and denied their cultures so that they could be more "American." When one group tries to become more like a larger, more powerful group, it is called *assimilation*.

A person can choose to change his or her culture. Changing one's race is usually not possible. No matter how "American" people of color become, racial discrimination continues. Multiculturalism helps us see some of the problems in our society that result from racial differences. *Antiracism*—working against racism—helps us solve those problems.

Maintaining racism costs a lot. It costs money and resources. Racism hurts everybody. That makes it everyone's job to fight racism. Being "tolerant" or "colorblind" or even "nonracist" really means ignor-

The Reverend Martin Luther King, Jr.: "If a man hasn't discovered something that he will die for, he isn't fit to live." (Courtesy of The Library of Congress)

ing racism—or sometimes even *being* racist. But ignoring racism won't make it go away.

Racism won't change unless people change it. Ending racism means working together to change laws, practices, behaviors, and attitudes. Martin Luther King, Jr. said, "The choice is ours, and though we might prefer it otherwise, we *must* choose." That choice beings with each individual.

It beings with you.

REVIEW QUESTIONS

1. Describe three steps students can take to fight racism inside their school.
2. Describe three steps students can take to fight racism outside their school.
3. Do you think multiculturalism is an answer to racism? How would it work in your city or town?

APPENDIX

RESOURCES

There are hundreds of organizations working to end racism. They range from big, national organizations to small groups of volunteers. Some concentrate on educating people about racism. Others try to change racist laws and practices. Still others work on issues such as poverty, unemployment, housing, and immigration. Often, these organizations work together.

Some of them, such as the NAACP and the American Indian Movement, have already been mentioned. Below are several more that can give you information, help you get involved with their projects, or put you in touch with other organizations.

You may already belong to a youth group through your school, community, or religious body. If your group is not already working on issues of racism, the organizations below may help you come up with some ideas for getting started.

American Friends Service Committee
1501 Cherry Street
Philadelphia, PA 19102
(215) 241–2700

Since 1917, the American Friends Service Committee (AFSC) has been devoted to building a just and peaceful world. In the book *Farewell to Manzanar*, Jeanne Wakatsuki Houston talks about the help her family received from AFSC when Japanese Americans were imprisoned during World War II. In 1947, AFSC was awarded a Nobel Peace Prize.

This independent Quaker organization works all over

the United States and in thirty other countries. It gives help to the victims of war. It encourages people to get involved in working for peace and justice. Many AFSC programs work against the effects of racism in American society. Others help adults and children resolve conflicts nonviolently.

AFSC has speakers, films, and literature on many different issues. It also works with other organizations. In many areas, AFSC helps organize youth groups.

Anti-Racism Survey Committee
Shael Polakow-Suransky
1312 South Forest
Ann Arbor, MI 48104

Shael Polakow-Suransky and other students developed a questionnaire on racism that was given to all high school students in Ann Arbor, Michigan. Their work resulted in a program for sixth graders called Students Educating Each Other About Discrimination (SEED). For a copy of the survey, send a self-addressed stamped envelope to Shael.

The Children's Museum
300 Congress Street
Boston, MA 02210-1034
(617) 426–6500

The Children's Museum is well known for the imaginative and fun ways in which it reflects Boston's (and the world's) racial and cultural diversity. "We're Still Here" is an exhibit about contemporary Indian people. "The Kid's Bridge" helps counter prejudice and racism by helping children learn about themselves and others. The Museum also features film series, cultural performances, storytelling, and many other activities. The Multicultural Project offers teacher training in multicultural and antiracist curriculum. Many resource materials are available from the museum.

Council on Interracial Books for Children, Inc.
1841 Broadway
New York, NY 10023
(212) 757–5339

The Council on Interracial Books for Children, Inc. (CIBC) is a nonprofit organization formed in 1965 by concerned editors, librarians, writers, and historians. They wanted to change the all-white world of children's book publishing. CIBI promotes literature for children that reflects a multi-cultural, multiracial society.

CIBC publishes the *Interracial Books for Children Bulletin.* This bulletin reviews children's books for racism, sexism, ageism, handicapism, and other antihuman values. It also provides articles on how these issues affect children's books and learning materials.

CIBC publishes books, pamphlets, and other materials that help students, parents, teachers, and librarians work against racism and sexism in education.

PERIODICALS

People of color often believe that their views are ignored or distorted in the popular media. Many have begun their own newspapers and magazines. In most cities with a large black population, you'll find newspapers written by and for African Americans. The same is true for Latinos, Asians, American Indians, and other people of color.

When you want to learn more about an issue, it is important to know how the people who are most affected by that issue feel about it. Remember, though, that no one source is the "final word" for any group of people. A Latino newspaper gives *a* Latino point of view, not *the* Latino point of view. An editorial in a Chinese magazine may express the opinion of *many* Chinese people, but not *all* Chinese people.

Established newspapers and magazines such as *Ebony*

may be available in your school or public library. Below are some periodicals that may be unfamiliar to you. They feature articles on current issues affecting people of color.

ABC, Americans Before Columbus
National Indian Youth Council
201 Hermosa, Northeast
Albuquerque, NM 87108

Akwesasne Notes (Native Peoples)
Mohawk Nation
via Rooseveltown, NY 13683

East West (Chinese American)
East/West Publishing Company
758 Commercial Street
San Francisco, CA 94108

El Grito: A Journal of Contemporary Mexican American Thought
Quinto Sol Publications
Box 9275
Berkeley, CA 94709

Emerge: Our Voice in Today's World (African American)
599 Broadway
New York, NY 10012

Urban Profile (African American)
215 Park Avenue South, Suite 1909
New York, NY 10003

Winds of Change: A Magazine of American Indians
1085 14th Street, Suite 1224
Boulder, CO 80302

NAMING RACES

People of color is a term that refers to all people whose ancestors were not white Europeans. In the United States, this includes African Americans, Asian Americans, Native Americans (Indians), and Latino Americans. *Whites* are people whose ancestors came from Europe. People who have only some European ancestry are usually regarded as people of color.

The term *people of color* has a long history. It was some-times used in nineteenth-century legal documents when a person's race was unknown. It was also widely used in other parts of the world, particularly by the British. Not everyone accepts this term, but it is still very useful. It is different from *colored*, a term that many people find offen-sive.

Asian refers to people from Japan, China, Korea, Viet-nam, and other countries in Asia. This group also includes people from the Pacific Islands, who may be called Pacific Islanders. *Oriental* is a term that many Asians find offen-sive.

Japanese who live in the United States but who were born in Japan call themselves *Issei*. Their children are called *Nisei*, and the third generation are called *Sansei*.

Blacks are people in the United States and the Caribbean whose ancestors came from Africa. Until the 1800s, most black people in the United States called themselves Afri-cans or African Americans. When whites tried to force free blacks out of the United States, black people stopped identifying with Africa. Instead they began to call them-selves colored. In public records, they were usually called negroes, from the Spanish word for black. *Negro*, capital-ized, was the term used most often in the twentieth cen-tury. Then, in the 1960s, along with the demand for Black Power came a pride in being black. *Black* became widely used. *Afro-American* and *African American* also came back into usage.

Black people come from many cultures and nations. Blacks who come to the United States from other places sometimes prefer being referred to by their nationality, such as Haitian or Dominican.

Hispanic is the term the U.S. government uses to refer to Spanish-speaking people from Central America, South America, and the Caribbean, and their descendants, who live in the United States. Many of them prefer the term *Latino*. It was created by the people themselves. They say it reflects a common cultural heritage (African, Indian, and Spanish) instead of just a common European language base. Females are called *Latinas*.

Puerto Ricans and Mexican Americans are the largest groups of Latinos. The United States took over the island of Puerto Rico in 1898. Puerto Ricans have been U.S. citizens since 1917. Many Mexican Americans call themselves Chicanos (or Chicanas). Like *Latino* the term *Chicano* reflects a pride in culture.

Indians are the descendants of the people who lived in the Americas thousands of years before Europeans arrived. They include Inuits (Eskimos) and Aleuts, the native people of Alaska. Indians are also referred to as American Indians, Native Americans, and Native Peoples. The U.S. government lists over 500 different Indian nations. Cherokee, Navajo, and Sioux are the three largest. The best way to refer to a native person is by his or her nation, if it is known.

All these categories include race, culture, and nationality. A person can belong to more than one group. For instance, a dark-skinned person from Puerto Rico may think of herself as black *and* Latina.

For many years, people of color have been called minorities or nonwhites. Many people have rejected those terms. *Nonwhite* is a negative term. Instead of saying what people are, it says what they are not. And *minority* isn't really accurate, because most of the world's people are dark skinned. Even in the United States, in your lifetime people of color will be the majority.

The English language is always changing. So are the names that people use to define themselves. Even people from the same racial group will have different preferences. How do you figure out how to refer to a person of a different race? The best way is to *ask that person*.

ORGANIZATIONS MENTIONED IN THIS BOOK

ADL. Anti-Defamation League of B'nai Brith, a Jewish education and advocacy organization.

AFL. American Federation of Labor; national organization of labor unions organized in 1881, later merged with CIO.

AIM. American Indian Movement; organized in 1968 to take militant protest action in support of Indian rights.

Black Panthers. Black militant group founded in Oakland, California in the 1960s, in response to police brutality against blacks.

Citizens' Councils. Known as the *white-collar Klan*, these groups were organized by southern whites to resist desegregation after the Supreme Court outlawed segregation.

CIO. Congress of Industrial Organizations; organized in 1935, later merged with AFL.

CORE. Congress of Racial Equality; civil rights group that began sit-ins in Chicago in 1942.

Crusade for Justice. Militant Chicano civil rights group organized in Denver in 1965.

FOR. Fellowship of Reconciliation; founded in 1914 to promote pacifism and international understanding.

Ku Klux Klan. White supremacist, terrorist organization founded in 1867 in Nashville, Tennessee.

La Raza Unida. "The race united"; Chicano political party organized in Texas in 1970.

NAACP. National Association for the Advancement of Colored People; founded in 1909 to work for legal rights of blacks.

Nation of Islam. Also known as *Black Muslims;* black religious organization that believes in racial separation.

Niagara Movement. The organization that preceded the NAACP.

OAAU. Organization of Afro-American Unity; founded by Malcolm X after his return from Mecca.

Red Guard. Militant organization of Chinese American youth; worked in California's Chinese communities in the 1970s.

SCLC. Southern Christian Leadership Conference; founded by a group of ministers to coordinate the civil rights movement.

SNCC. Student Nonviolent Coordinating Committee; civil rights group that did voter registration and civil protest in the 1960s.

UFW. United Farm Workers; the first agricultural union in the United States; began organizing in 1962.

SLAVERY LAWS IN VIRGINIA, 1639–1705

Compiled by Robert Bellinger, Department of History, Suffolk University, Boston, Massachusetts

1639 Act X: "All persons except Negroes are to be provided with arms and ammunition or be fined at the pleasure of the governor and council."

1642 A statute is passed that requires those servants brought to the colony without indenture to serve four years if older than twenty of age, five years if between twelve and twenty, and seven years if under twelve.

1654 Act XVI: "Dutch and all strangers of Christian nations are allowed free trade if they give bond and pay import of ten shillings per hogshead laid upon all tobacco exported to any foreign dominion; always provided that if Dutch or other foreigners shall import any Negro slaves they, the said Dutch or other foreigners, shall for the tobacco really produced by the said Negroes, pay only the impost of two shillings per hogshead, the like being paid by our own nation."

1660 Act XXII: "It is enacted that in case any English servant shall run away in company with any Negroes who are incapable of making satisfaction by addition of time that the English so running away shall serve for the time of the Negroes absence as they are to do for their own by a former act."

1662 A statute is passed saying "each woman servant got with child by her master shall after her indenture is expired be sold for two years by the church wardens, the tobacco to be employed by the vestry for the use of the parish."

Act XII: "Children got by an Englishman upon a Negro woman shall be bond or free according to the condition of the mother, and if any Christian shall commit fornication with a Negro man or woman, he shall pay double the fines of a former act."

1667 Act III: "Whereas some doubts have arisen whether children that are slaves by birth, and by the charity of their owners made partners of the blessed sacrament of baptism, should by virtue of their baptism be made free, it is enacted that baptism does not alter the condition of the person as to his bondage of freedom; masters, freed from this doubt may more carefully propagate Christianity by permitting slaves to be admitted to that sacrament."

1669 An act about the casual killing of slaves: "Whereas the only law in force for the punishment of refractory servants resisting their master, mistress or overseer, cannot be inflicted on Negroes, nor the obstinacy of many of them by other than violent means supprest. Be it enacted and declared by this grand assembly, if any slave resist his master . . . and by the extremity of the correction should chance to die, that his death shall not be accompted Felony, but the master (or that person appointed by the master to punish him) be acquit from molestation, since it cannot be presumed that propensed malice (which alone makes murther Felony) should induce any man to destroy his own estate."

1670 An act is passed that divides non-Christian servants into two classes: "those imported into this colony by shipping, who 'shall be slaves for their lives'; and those who 'shall come by land,' who 'shall serve, if boys or girls, until thirty years of age; if men or women twelve years and no longer.' '

[In 1682, all imported non-Christians were made slaves.]

1680 Act X: "Whereas the frequent meetings of considerable numbers of Negro slaves under pretense of feasts and burials is judged of dangerous consequence (it is) enacted that no Negro or slave may carry arms, such as any club, staff, gun, sword, or other weapon, nor go from his owner's plantation without a certificate and then only on necessary occasions; the punishment twenty lashes on the bare back, well laid on. And further, if any Negro lift up his hand against any Christian he shall receive thirty lashes, and if he absent himself or lie out from his master's service and resist lawful apprehension, he may be killed and this law shall be published every six months."

1691 Act XVI: "Whatsoever English or other white man or woman, bond or free, shall intermarry with a Negro, mulatto, or Indian man or woman, bond or free, he shall within three months be banished from this dominion forever.

"And it is further enacted, that if any English woman being free shall have a bastard child by a Negro she shall play fifteen pounds to the church wardens, and in default of such payment, she shall be taken into possession by the church wardens and disposed of for five years and the amount she brings shall be paid one-third to their majesties for the support of the government, one-third to the warden of the parish where the offense is committed and the other third to the informer. The child shall be bound out by the church wardens until he is thirty years of age. In case the English woman that shall have a bastard is a servant she shall be sold by the church wardens (after her time is expired) for five years, and the child serve as aforesaid."

1705 Chapter XXIII: "All Negro, mulatto, and Indian slaves within the dominion shall be held to be real estate and not chattels and shall descend unto heirs and widow according to the custom of land inheritance, and be held in 'free simple'. . . . Nothing in this act shall be construed to give the owner of a slave not seized of other real estate the right to vote as a freeholder."

Chapter XXXIV: "And if any slave resist his master, or owner, or other person, by his or her older, correcting such slave, and shall happen to be killed in such correction, shall be free and acquit of all punishment and accusation for the same, as if such accident had never happened."

Chapter XXXVIII: "Provided always, and it is further enacted, that for every slave killed, in pursuance of this act, or put to death by law, the master or owner of such slave shall be paid by the public."

LETTER FROM BIRMINGHAM JAIL

April 16, 1963

My Dear Fellow Clergymen:

While confined here in the Birmingham city jail, I came across your recent statement calling my present activities "unwise and untimely." Seldom do I pause to answer criticism of my work and ideas. If I sought to answer all the criticisms that cross my desk, my secretaries would have little time for anything other than such correspondence in the course of the day, and I would have no time for constructive work. But since I feel that you are men of genuine good will and that your criticisms are sincerely set forth, I want to try to answer your statement in what I hope will be patient and reasonable terms.

I think I should indicate why I am here in Birmingham, since you have been influenced by the view which argues against "outsiders coming in." I have the honor of serving as president of the Southern Christian Leadership Conference, an organization operating in every southern state, with headquarters in Atlanta, Georgia. We have some eighty-five affiliated organizations across the South, and one of them is the Alabama Christian Movement for Human Rights. Frequently we share staff, educational and financial resources with our affiliates. Several months ago the affiliate here in Birmingham asked us to be on call to engage in a nonviolent direct-action program if such were deemed necessary. We readily consented, and when the hour came we lived up to our promise. So I, along with several members of my staff, am here because I was invited here. I am here because I have organizational ties here.

But more basically, I am in Birmingham because injustice is here. Just as the prophets of the eighth century B.C. left their villages and carried their "thus saith the Lord" far beyond the boundaries of their home towns, and just as the Apostle Paul left his village of Tarsus and carried the gospel of Jesus Christ to the far corners of the Greco-Roman world, so am I compelled to carry the gospel of freedom beyond my own home town. Like Paul, I must constantly respond to the Macedonian call for aid.

Moreover, I am cognizant of the interrelatedness of all communities and states. I cannot sit idly by in Atlanta and not be concerned about what happens in Birmingham. Injustice anywhere is a threat to justice everywhere. We are caught in an inescapable network of mutuality, tied in a single garment of destiny. Whatever affects one directly, affects all indirectly. Never again can we afford to live with the narrow, provincial "outsider agitator" idea. Anyone who lives inside the United States can never be considered an outsider anywhere within its bounds.

You deplore the demonstrations taking place in Birmingham. But your statement, I am sorry to say, fails to express a similar concern for the conditions that brought about the demonstrations. I am sure that none of you would want to rest content with the superficial kind of social analysis that deals merely with effects and does not grapple with underlying causes. It is unfortunate that demonstrations are taking place in Birmingham, but it is even more unfortunate that the city's white power structure left the Negro community with no alternative.

In any nonviolent campaign there are four basic steps: collection of the facts to determine whether injustices exist; negotiation; self-purification; and direct action. We have gone through all these steps in Birmingham. There can be no gainsaying the fact that racial injustice engulfs this community. Birmingham is probably the most thoroughly segregated city in the United States. Its ugly record of brutality is widely known. Negroes have experienced grossly unjust treatment in the courts. There have been more unsolved bombings of Negro homes and churches in Birmingham than in any other city in the nation. These are the hard, brutal facts of the case. On the basis of these conditions, Negro leaders sought to negotiate with the city fathers. But the latter consistently refused to engage in good-faith negotiation.

You may well ask: "Why direct action? Why sit-ins, marches and so forth? Isn't negotiation a better path?" You are quite right in calling for negotiation. Indeed, this is the very purpose of direct action. Nonviolent direct action seeks to create such a crisis and foster such a tension that a community which has constantly refused to negotiate is forced to confront the issue. It seeks so to dramatize the issue that it can no longer be ignored. My citing the creation of tension as part of the work of the nonviolent-resister may sound rather shocking. But I must confess that I am not afraid of the word "tension." I have earnestly opposed violent tension, but there is a type of constructive, nonviolent tension which is necessary for growth. Just as Socrates felt that it was necessary to create a tension in the mind so that individuals could rise from the bondage of myths and half-truths to the unfettered realm of creative analysis and objective appraisal, so must we see the need for nonviolent gadflies to create the kind of tension in society that will help men rise from the dark depths of prejudice and racism to the majestic heights of under-standing and brotherhood.

The purpose of our direct-action program is to create a situation so crisis-packed that it will inevitably open the door to negotiation. I therefore concur with you in your call for negotiation. Too long has our beloved Southland been bogged down in a tragic effort to live in monologue rather than dialogue.

We have waited for more than 340 years for our constitutional and God-given rights. The nations of Asia and Africa are moving with jetlike speed toward gaining political independence, but we still creep at horse-and-buggy pace toward gaining a cup of coffee at a lunch counter. Perhaps it is easy for those who have never felt the stinging darts of segregation to say, "Wait." But when you have seen vicious mobs lynch your mothers and fathers at will and drown your sisters and brothers at whim; when you have seen hate-filled policemen curse, kick and even kill your black brothers and sisters; when you see the vast majority of your twenty million Negro brothers smothering in an airtight cage of poverty in the midst of an affluent society; when you suddenly find your tongue twisted and your speech stammering as you seek to explain to your six-year-old daughter why she can't go to the public amusement park that has just been advertised on television, and see tears welling up in her eyes when she is told that Funtown is closed to colored children, and see ominous clouds of inferiority beginning to form in her little mental sky, and see her beginning to distort her personality by developing an unconscious bitterness toward white people; when you have to concoct an answer for a five-year-old son who is asking: "Daddy, why do white people treat colored people so mean?"; when you take a cross-country drive and find it necessary to sleep night after night in the uncomfortable corners of your automobile because no motel will accept you; when you are humiliated day in and day out by nagging signs reading "white" and "colored"; when your first name becomes "nigger," your middle name becomes "boy" (however old you are) and your last name becomes "John," and your wife and mother are never given the respected title "Mrs."; when you are harried by day and haunted by night by the fact that you are a Negro, living constantly at tiptoe stance, never quite knowing what to expect next, and are plagued with inner fears and outer resentments; when you are forever fighting a degenerating sense of "nobodiness"—then you will understand why we find it difficult to wait. There comes a time when the cup of endurance runs over, and men are no longer willing to be plunged into the abyss of despair. I hope, sirs, you can understand our legitimate and unavoidable impatience.

I must make two honest confessions to you, my Christian and Jewish brothers. First, I must confess that over the past few years I have been gravely disappointed with the white moderate. I have almost reached the regrettable conclusion that the Negro's great stumbling block in his stride toward freedom is not the White Citizen's Counciler or the Ku Klux Klanner, but the white moderate, who is more devoted to "order" than to justice; who prefers a negative peace which is the absence of tension to a positive peace which is the presence of justice; who constantly says: "I agree with you in the goal you seek, but I cannot agree with your methods of direct action"; who paternalistically believes he can set the timetable for another man's freedom; who lives by a mythical concept of time and who constantly advises the Negro to wait for a "more convenient season." Shallow understanding from people of good will is more frustrating than absolute misunderstanding from people of ill will. Lukeward acceptance is much more bewildering than outright rejection.

I had hoped that the white moderate would understand that law and order exist for the purpose of establishing justice and that when they fail in this purpose they become the dangerously structured dams that block the flow of social progress. I had hoped that the white moderate would understand that the present tension in the South is a necessary phase of the transition from an obnoxious negative peace, in which the Negro passively accepted his unjust plight, to a substantive and positive peace, in which all men will respect the dignity and worth of human personality. Actually, we who engage in nonviolent direct action are not the creators of tension. We merely bring to the surface the hidden tension that is already alive. We bring it out in the open, where it can be seen and dealt with. Like a boil that can never be cured so long as it is covered up but must be opened with all its ugliness to the natural medicines of air and light, injustice must be exposed, with all the tension its exposure creates, to the light of human conscience and the air of national opinion before it can be cured.

Oppressed people cannot remain oppressed forever. The yearning for freedom eventually manifests itself, and that is what has happened to the American negro. Something within has reminded him of his birthright of freedom, and something without has reminded him that it can be gained. Consciously or unconsciously, he has been caught up by the *Zeitgeist,* and with his black brothers of Africa and his brown and yellow brothers of Asia, South America and the Caribbean, the United States Negro is moving with a sense of great urgency toward the promised land of racial justice. If one recognizes this vital urge that has engulfed the Negro community, one should readily understand why public demonstrations are taking place. The Negro has many pent-up resentments and latent frustrations, and he must release them. So let him march; let him make prayer pilgrimages to the city hall; let him go on freedom rides— and try to understand why he must do so. If his repressed emotions are not released in nonviolent ways, they will seek expression through violence; this is not a threat but a fact of history. So I have not said to my people: "Get rid of your discontent." Rather, I have tried to say that this normal and healthy discontent can be channeled into the creative outlet of nonviolent direct action. And now this approach is being termed extremist.

Let me take note of my other major disappointment. I have been so greatly disappointed with the white church and its leadership. Of course, there are some notable exceptions. I am not unmindful of the fact that each of you has taken some significant stands on this issue. I commend you, Reverend Stallings, for your Christian stand on this past Sunday, in welcoming Negroes to your worship service on a nonsegregated basis. I commend the Catholic leaders of this state for integrating Spring Hill College several years ago.

But despite these notable exceptions, I must honestly reiterate that I have been disappointed with the church. I do not say this as one of those negative critics who can always find something wrong with the church. I say this as a minister of the gospel, who loves the church; who was nurtured in its bosom; who has been sustained by its spiritual blessings and who will remain true to it as long as the cord of life shall lengthen.

When I was suddenly catapulted into the leadership of the bus protest in Montgomery, Alabama, a few years ago, I felt we would be supported by the white church. I felt that the white ministers, priests and rabbis of the South would be among our strongest allies. Instead, some have been outright opponents, refusing to understand the freedom movement and misrepresenting its leaders; all too many others have been more cautious than courageous and have remained silent behind the anesthetizing security of stained-glass windows.

In spite of my shattered dreams, I came to Birmingham with the hope that the white religious leadership of this community would see the justice of our cause and, with deep moral concern, would serve as the channel through which our just grievances could reach the power structure. I had hoped that each of you would understand. But again I have been disappointed.

I have heard numerous southern religious leaders admonish their worshipers to comply with a desegregation decision because it is the law, but I have longed to hear white ministers declare: "Follow this decree because integration is morally right and because the Negro is your brother." In the midst of blatant injustices inflicted upon the Negro, I have watched white churchmen stand on the sideline and mouth pious irrelevancies and sanctimonious trivialities. In the midst of a mighty struggle to rid our nation of racial and economic injustice, I have heard many ministers say: "Those are social issues, with which the gospel has no real concern." And I have watched many churches commit themselves to a completely otherworldly religion which makes a strange, un-Biblical distinction between body and soul, between the sacred and the secular.

Before closing I feel impelled to mention one other point in your statement that has troubled me profoundly. You warmly commended the Birmingham police force for keeping "order" and "preventing violence." I doubt that you would have so warmly commended the police force if you had seen its dogs sinking their teeth into unarmed, nonviolent Negroes. I doubt that you would so quickly commend the policemen if you were to observe their ugly and inhumane treatment of Negroes here in the city jail; if you were to watch them push and curse old Negro women and young Negro girls; if you were to see them slap and kick old Negro men and young boys; if you were to observe them, as they did on two occasions, refuse to give us food because we wanted to sing our grace together. I cannot join you in your praise of the Birmingham police department.

It is true that the police have exercised a degree of discipline in handling the demonstrators. In this sense they have conducted themselves rather "nonviolently" in public. But for what purpose? To preserve the evil system of segregation. Over the past few years I have consistently preached that nonviolence demands that the means we use must be as pure as the ends we seek. I have tried to make clear that it is wrong to use immoral means to attain moral ends. But now I must affirm that it is just as wrong, or perhaps even more so, to use moral means to preserve immoral ends. Perhaps Mr. Connor and his policemen have been rather nonviolent in public, as was Chief Pritchett in Albany, Georgia, but they have used the moral means of nonviolence to maintain the immoral end of racial injustice. As T. S. Eliot has said: "The last temptation is the greatest treason: To do the right deed for the wrong reason."

Never before have I written so long a letter. I'm afraid it is much too long to take your precious time. I can assure you that it would have been much shorter if I had been writing from a comfortable desk, but what else can one do when he is alone in a narrow jail cell, other than write long letters, think long thoughts and pray long prayers?

If I have said anything in this letter that overstates the truth and indicates an unreasonable impatience, I beg you to forgive me. If I have said anything that understates the truth and indicates my having a patience that allows me to settle for anything less than brotherhood, I beg God to forgive me.

I hope this letter finds you strong in the faith. I also hope that circumstances will soon make it possible for me to meet each of you, not as an integrationist or a civil-rights leader but as a fellow clergyman and a Christian brother. Let us all hope that the dark clouds of racial prejudice will soon pass away and the deep fog of misunderstanding will be lifted from our fear-drenched communities, and in some not too distant tomorrow the radiant stars of love and brotherhood will shine over our great nation with all their scintillating beauty.

Yours for the cause of Peace and Brotherhood,
MARTIN LUTHER KING, JR.

BEYOND VIETNAM

Excerpted from a speech given by Martin Luther King, Jr., to Clergy and Laymen Concerned About Vietnam, Riverside Church, New York City, April 4, 1967.

Over the past two years, as I have moved to break the betrayal of my own silences and to speak from the burnings of my own heart, as I have called for radical departures from the destruction of Vietnam, many persons have questioned me about the wisdom of my path. At the heart of their concerns this query has often loomed large and loud: Why are *you* speaking about the war, Dr. King: Why are *you* joining the voices of dissent? Peace and civil rights don't mix, they say. Aren't you hurting the cause of your own people, they ask? And when I hear them, though I often understand the sources of their concern, I am nevertheless greatly saddened, for such questions mean that the inquirers have not really known me, my commitment or my calling. Indeed, their questions suggest that they do not know the world in which they live.

Since I am a preacher by trade, I suppose it is not surprising that I have several reasons for bringing Vietnam into the field of my moral vision. There is at the outset a very obvious and almost facile connection between the war in Vietnam and the struggle I, and others, have been waging in America. A few years ago there was a shining moment in that struggle. It seemed as if there was a real promise of hope for the poor—both black and white— through the Poverty Program. There were experiments, hopes, new beginnings. Then came the build-up in Vietnam and I watched the program broken and eviscerated as if it were some idle political plaything of a society gone mad on war, and I knew that America would never invest the necessary funds or energies in rehabilitation of its poor so long as adventures like Vietnam continued to draw men and skills and money like some demoniacal destructive suction tube. So I was increasingly compelled to see the war as an enemy of the poor and to attack it as such.

Perhaps the more tragic recognition of reality took place when it became clear to me that the war was doing far more than devastating the hopes of the poor at home. It was sending their sons and their brothers and their husbands to fight and to die in extraordinarily high proportions relative to the rest of the population. We were taking the black young men who had been crippled by our society and sending them 8,000 miles away to guarantee liberties in Southeast Asia which they had not found in Southwest Georgia and East Harlem. So we have been repeatedly faced with the cruel irony of watching Negro and white boys on TV screens as they kill and die together for a nation that has been unable to seat them together in the same schools. So we watch them in brutal solidarity burning the huts of a poor village but we realize that they would never live in the same block in Detroit. I could not be silent in the face of such cruel manipulation of the poor.

My third reason moves to an even deeper level of awareness, for it grows out of my experience in the ghettos of the north over the last three years—especially the last three summers. As I have walked among the desperate, rejected and angry young men I have told them that Molotov cocktails and rifles would not solve their problems. I have tried to offer them my deepest compassion while maintaining my conviction that social change comes most meaningfully through non-violent action. But they asked—and rightly so—what about Vietnam? They asked if our nation wasn't using massive doses of violence to solve its problems, to bring about the changes it wanted. Their questions hit home, and I knew that I could never again raise my voice against the violence of the oppressed in the ghettos without having first spoken clearly to the greatest purveyor of violence in the world today—my own government. For the sake of those boys, for the sake of this government, for the sake of hundreds of thousands trembling under our violence, I cannot be silent.

STATEMENT TO THE PEOPLE OF THE UNITED STATES AND THE WORLD

Excerpted from a joint position paper issued by the Dine (Navajo), Lakota (Sioux), and Haudenosaunee (Six Nations of the Iroquois Confederacy), July 1978.

The basic issue of Human Rights raised by the President of the U.S. is hypocrisy and an outrage when viewed in the context of the history and present conditions of our peoples.

The definition of Genocide as stated in Article II of the International Convention on Genocide provides the basis of our peoples' charge of Genocide made at the United Nations in Geneva, Switzerland, in September, 1977.

Article II states: "In the present Convention, genocide means any of the following acts committed with intent to destroy, in whole or in part, a national, ethnical, racial, or religious group, such as.

(a) Killing members of the group;
(b) Causing serious bodily or mental harm to members of the group
(c) Deliberately inflicting on the group conditions of life calculated to bring about its physical destruction in whole or in part;
(d) Imposing measures intended to prevent births within the group."

Many of our young people went across the seas and never returned. We were told that we went to war to fight for our country. Our war casualties under the U.S. flag are greater than any other sector of the North American population. Yet today, our country is threatened by the U.S.

U.S. police and intelligence agencies have directed illegal military operations against our peoples, such as COINTEL-PRO. These actions have resulted in the violent deaths of a number of our leaders. The process has not stopped, and we have no protection against these actions. As a result of these actions there are in many U.S. prisons patriotic Native People who only advocate peace and freedom for their nations.

According to a GAO report issued last year, 24% of our women were forcibly or illegally sterilized during the period 1971–1975.

Nearly one out of three of our children are being placed in non-Indian foster homes daily by various county, state and federal agencies.

The Indian Reorganization Act of 1934 continues to destroy the traditional governments of our people, causing widespread disruption of a tranquil Way of Life, and literally putting brother against brother.

The clearcut policy of genocide of the last century continues in more sophisticated forms in this century.

Our religions have been attacked, and degraded. Our children continue to be processed through various forms of Western educational programs. The Spiritual leaders of our nations are now being subjected to the destructive nature of government program moneys. Taxpayers' moneys are being used to regulate the practice of our natural religions. There are even efforts to certify our medicine peoples and to despiritualize the nature of our healing culture. That practice is a policy which is an outrageous attempt to intefere with, and ultimately destroy our natural religion.

Finally, the bills currently before Congress which call for the abrogation of Indian treaties, and termination of our lands, resources, and water, present a clear signal that the threat of genocide to the existence of our peoples is alive and well. The fact that the present Congress of the U.S., in the year 1978, can consider such legislation should alarm the people of the U.S. When a government denies the human rights of one people, it is only a matter of time before those rights will be denied to all of its peoples.

We call upon the voting public of the U.S. to seriously consider and question the ethics and morality of their representative leadership in Congress who are responsible for the introduction of dangerous and racist legislation against our peoples.

We call upon the U.S. to acknowledge its responsibilities under international law to respect Indian treaties, to insure genuine self-determination for our nations, and to correct past wrongs in an honorable and equitable manner.

The traditional people recognize that the injustices perpetuated upon our people, and indeed upon many of the peoples of the world, are the major factors destroying the Spirituality of the Human Race. Peace and Unity are the foundations of the Spiritual Way of Life of our peoples. But Peace and Unity are not companions to injustice.

We call upon all the peoples of the world to join with us in seeking peace, and in seeking to insure survival and justice for all indigenous peoples, for all the Earth's creatures, and all nations of the Earth.

We will take whatever steps necessary in the protection of our Sacred Mother Earth, and the rights and well-being of our peoples.

We will continue our efforts before the World Community to regain our inherent Human and Sovereign Rights.

GLOSSARY

Abolition. A movement begun in the eighteenth century to end slavery.

Affirmative action. A policy that requires organizations to consider race, sex, and ethnicity in making decisions.

Anglo. A person of European ancestry; a white person. Used mostly in the Southwest.

Anti-Semitism. Prejudice or discrimination against Jews.

Apartheid. South Africa's official policy of racial segregation.

Assiento. An agreement that gave England the right to supply Spanish America with slaves from 1713 to 1743.

Bantustan. In South Africa, the areas set aside for blacks; also called *homelands*.

Black and Blues. Black Union army troops in the 1860s and 1870s.

Black Cabinet. President Franklin Roosevelt's black advisers.

Black Codes. Laws enacted after the Civil War to oppress blacks.

Black Power. A term used in the 1960s that called for blacks to control their own institutions and lives.

Civil rights movement. Campaigns during the 1950s and 1960s to gain equal protection under the law for blacks.

Class. A group of people with similar social, economic, and cultural status.

Conquistadores. Spanish adventurers who invaded

Central and South America in the sixteenth and seventeenth centuries.

Criollos. Mexican descendants of the Spanish, considered whites.

Discrimination. Actions based on prejudice.

Emigration. Leaving one region or country to settle in another.

Exodus of 1879. The massive migration of blacks from southern states.

Fifteenth Amendment. Guaranteed the right to vote to all male citizens.

Five Civilized Tribes. Cherokee, Choctaw, Chickasaw, Creek, and Seminole Indians.

Fourteenth Amendment. Guaranteed equal protection under the law to all citizens.

Freedman's Bureau. A government agency established after the Civil War to help former slaves.

Freedom Ride. Bus trips made by biracial groups of students through the segregated South in the 1960s.

Home rule. The demand by southern states for withdrawal of federal troops in 1877; in recent past, has referred to the demand by residents of Washington, D.C. for political self-determination.

Indentured servants. Immigrants who sold their services for a specific number of years in exchange for passage to the United States.

Institutional racism. A system that provides advantages to one race of people at the expense of another.

Integration. Inclusion of all races and ethnic groups without restriction.

Internment. Imprisonment during a time of war; specifically, of the Japanese during World War II.

Jim Crow. Southern segregation laws in the nineteenth and twentieth centuries.

Manifest Destiny. The belief that Europeans and their descendants were chosen by God to rule all of the Americas.

Mestizos. Mexican descendants of the Spanish and Indians.

Nativism. A movement designed to restrict immigration to America and protect the interests of native-born whites.

Outlyers. Bands of escaped slaves who formed settlements and attacked nearby plantations.

Prejudice. An opinion formed about someone or something without knowing the facts.

Reconstruction. The ten-year period following the Civil War, during which southern blacks participated in local, state, and federal government.

Red Sticks. A group of Creek Indians who fought against the United States during the War of 1812 and the Creek War of 1813–14.

Red Summer of 1919. So-called because of twenty-six race riots and numerous attacks on blacks.

Reservation. Land set aside by the federal government for an Indian nation.

Segregation. Separation in housing, education, industry, etc., that discriminates by race.

Slave Codes. Southern laws that controlled black slaves.

Thirteenth Amendment. Abolished slavery in the United States.

Trail of Tears. The forced removal of Cherokee Indians from Georgia in 1838.

Treaty. An agreement between two nations.

BIBLIOGRAPHY

ARTICLES

Bagasao, Paula Y. "Student Voices Breaking the Silence: The Asian and Pacific American Experience." *Change*, November/December 1989.

Bennett, Arlene P. "Eugenics as a Vital Part of Institutionalized Racism." In *A Freedomways Reader: Afro-America in the Seventies*. International Publishers, New York, 1977.

Burns, Haywood. "Racism in American Law." In *Amistad Two*. Vintage Books, New York, 1971.

Carson, Carol G., and Crosby, Faye J. "RX: Affirmative Action." *Smith Alumnae Quarterly*, Winter 1989.

Denton, Nancy A., and Massey, Douglas S. "Residential Segregation of Blacks, Hispanics, and Asians by Socioeconomic Status and Generation." *Social Science Quarterly*, December 1988.

Henry, William A., III. "Beyond the Melting Pot." *Time*, April 9, 1990.

Holmes, Steven. "Retreat on Civil Rights?" *American Visions*, October 1989.

Moore, Robert B. "Two Hundred Years of White Racism: No Cause for Celebration." Paper presented at Equity in an Era of Diversity Conference, Philadelphia, August 19, 1987.

Polakow-Suransky, Shael, and Ulaby, Neda. "Students Take Action to Combat Racism." *Phi Deltan Kappan*, April 1990.

Roper, Burns W. "Race Relations in America." *Christian Science Monitor*, July 13, 1990.

Smith, Vernon E. "The Vanishing Rainbow: Hate Crimes on the Rise." *Emerge*, August 1990.

Trescott, Jacqueline. "Fate, Hope and the Black Child." *Emerge*, May 1990.

Tye, Larry. "Hate Crimes on Rise in U.S." *Boston Globe*, August 1990.

BOOKS

Aptheker, Herbert, ed. *A Documentary History of The Negro People in the United States*, 1910–1932. Secaucus, N.J., Citadel Press, 1973.

Banks, James, ed. *Teaching Strategies for Ethnic Studies*. Boston, Allyn and Bacon, 1975.

Bennett, Lerone Jr. *Before the Mayflower: A History of Black America*. New York, Penguin Books, 1982.

Bernal, Martin. *Black Athena: The Afro-Asiatic Roots of Classical Civilization*, volume 1. New Brunswick, N.J., Rutgers University Press, 1987.

Blaustein, Albert P., and Zangrando, Robert L. *Civil Rights and the Black American: A Documentary History*. New York, Washington Square Press, 1968.

Bogle, Donald. *Toms, Coons, Mulattoes, Mammies, and Bucks*. New York, Bantam Books, 1974.

Brown, Dee. *Bury My Heart At Wounded Knee*. New York, Washington Square Press, 1981.

Burnette, Robert, and Koster, John. *The Road to Wounded Knee*. New York, Bantam Books, 1974.

Chronicles of American Indian Protest. New York, Council on Interracial Books for Children, 1979.

Du Bois, W. E. B. *The Souls of Black Folk*. New York, Bantam Books, 1989.

Freedom Now! *Can't Jail the Spirit: Political Prisoners in the U.S.* Chicago, Editorial El Coqui, 1988.

Gonzales, Rudolfo. *I Am Joaquin*. New York, Bantam Books, 1972.

Harding, Vincent. *There Is A River: The Black Struggle for Freedom in America*. New York, Vintage, 1983.

Hodgkinson, Harold L. *All One System: Demographics of Education—Kindergarten Through Graduate School*. Washington, D.C., Institute for Educational Leadership, 1985.

Horne, Gerald, ed. *Thinking and Rethinking U.S. History.* New York, Council on Interracial Books for Children, 1988.

Houston, Jeanne Wakatsuki, and Houston, James D. *Farewell to Manzanar.* New York, Bantam Books, 1972.

Jackson, Florence. *The Black Man in America, 1932–1954.* New York, Franklin Watts, n.d.

Lomax, Louis E. *To Kill A Black Man.* Los Angeles, Holloway House, 1987.

Matthiessen, Peter. *In the Spirit of Crazy Horse.* New York, Viking, 1983.

Pevar, Stephen L. *The Rights of Indians and Tribes.* New York, Bantam Books, 1983.

President's Advisory Commission on Civil Disorders. *Report of the National Advisory Commission on Civil Disorders.* New York, Bantam Books, 1968.

Shakur, Assata. *Assata: An Autobiography.* Westport, Conn., Lawrence Hill, 1987.

Thomas, Alexander, and Sillen, Samuel. *Racism and Psychiatry.* Secaucus, N.J., Citadel Press, 1972.

Van Sertima, Ivan. *They Came Before Columbus: The African Presence in Ancient America.* New York, Random House, 1976.

Weatherford, Jack M. *Indian Givers: How the Indians of the Americas Transformed the World.* New York, Crown, 1988.

Williams, Juan. *Eyes On the Prize: America's Civil Rights Years, 1954–1965.* New York, Viking Penguin, 1987.

Zinn, Howard. *A People's History of the United States.* New York, Harper Colophon Books, 1980.

INDEX